YOUR DAILY DOSE of QUOTES & ANECDOTES II

PRAISE FOR BOB LEE

We're living in times that have all of us discussing the future of America. Terrorism, Race, International Trade, Global Recessions and Politics have us all on edge these days. But I firmly believe our greatest challenge in America today involves the education of our children. Our kids continue to face challenges from both home and classroom that are unprecedented.

Roadblocks to learning are everywhere, yet solutions to improving public education in our inner-cities start with listening to our children. They're speaking louder than ever but most of us don't hear them. However, our own Bob Lee is quite the exception. He's been listening to our children for decades, meeting them in school, on the playground, hosting their dances and sporting events, while encouraging them every step of the way.

From the Bronx to Brooklyn, Newark to Westchester; Bob Lee is a testament to the power of Media when it touches people in the communities they live in. Bob has a message from both teachers and students that can provide us all valuable lessons that will lead to re-thinking our current system of testing and blaming teachers when the scores don't measure up to expectation.

Bob's "Make the Grade" Foundation is all about accountability, but there's a heck of a lot of fun and learning along the way I've seldom seen in the numerous programs I've encountered in Public School systems including: Brooklyn, Buffalo, Detroit and New Orleans LA.

Grab a cup of coffee or tea with me, open the book and let's take a lesson from the many diverse voices of our children, dedicated teachers, parents, community activists, clergy, and celebrities as told by Bob Lee....

Skip Dillard
WBLS/WLIB New York

YOUR DAILY DOSE of QUOTES & ANECDOTES II

Featuring
WORDS of WISDOM
To Help You
MAKE the GRADE

WITH
BONUS SECTION

DOCTOR BOB LEE
WITH
YVONNE ROSE

BOB LEE ENTERPRISES
New York City

YOUR DAILY DOSE of
QUOTES & ANECDOTES II

Published by
Bob Lee Enterprises
Make the Grade Foundation
244 Madison Avenue, #500
New York, NY 10016
Makethegrade4u@gmail.com
www.makethegrade.org

Bob Lee, Publisher & Editorial Director
Yvonne Rose, Editor
QualityPress.info, Production Coordinator

ALL RIGHTS RESERVED

No part of this book may be reproduced or transmitted in any form or by any means – electronic or mechanical, including photocopying, recording or by any information storage and retrieved system without written permission from the authors, except for the inclusion of brief quotations in a review.

Bob Lee Enterprises' books are available at special discounts for bulk purchases, sales promotions, fund raising or educational purposes.

© copyright 2018 by Bob Lee
ISBN #: 978-0-9970948-3-1
Library of Congress Control #: 2018910676

DEDICATION

To the women and men who take the time to uplift our children by demonstrating positive thoughts, words and deeds that provide a firm foundation for the betterment of our communities and the people that dwell in them.

CONTENTS

FOREWORD 1
INTRODUCTION 5

PART ONE : SEVEN MOTIVATING PRINCIPLES 7
ONE : Parents 9
TWO : The Teacher 25
THREE : The Student 38
FOUR : The Community 54
FIVE : Spirituality 68
SIX : Health 88
SEVEN : Financial Literacy 101

PART TWO : MEMORABLE QUOTES
                WITH MEANINGFUL MESSAGES 115
Preparation 117
Inspiration 120
Change 124
Forgiveness 128
Acceptance 130
Success 133
Challenges 136
Confidence 142
Integrity 145
Love and Friendship 150

PART THREE : DOCTOR BOB'S TOP 120
                 FAN FAVE QUOTES 157

PART FOUR : BONUS SECTION 169
    Just For Fun… 15 Memorable Movie Lines 171
    Quotes Meant To Motivate You 172
    Quotes To Help Keep You On Course 175
    Quotes That Challenge Your Power Within 177
    Quotes That Create Awareness 180
    Quotes That Make You Think Twice 183
    Quotes That Emphasize Black Awareness 186
    Notable Quotes To Stimulate Your Thoughts 187
IN CONCLUSION 189
ABOUT THE AUTHOR 193
YOUR FAVORITE QUOTE(S) 196

FOREWORD

When I initially learned that Bob Lee's second literary foray was going to be a book of his favorite quotes, I will admit that I was a bit skeptical. By that, I said to myself *'many authors have had collections of sayings from Confucius to President Barak Obama'* and I simultaneously asked myself, *'how would this be a unique experience to the reader and reach a wide audience?* The more I thought of it, the more it made sense. For one, Bob and I have been close for over forty years and thinking back to my earliest memories of him and the entire Lee family, it was easy to see that if there was anything that helped drive them as a family, other than love, it was quotes and anecdotes! And then it clicked. This would not just be any old book of quotes. This would be a book about the pillars in which Bob and the Lee family were built upon.

The all-encompassing "they" have always said that hindsight is twenty-twenty and of course "they" are always correct. In writing this introduction it became all too clear that I have used these family quotes and anecdotes to guide my adult life and young family. I regularly find myself repeating a number of them when guiding my three children. When paired down, two quotes usually stand out in my mind. The first being:

"What you *are*, is GOD's gift to you. What you *make* of yourself, is your gift to GOD. So choose your *choice* and let your *choice* control the chooser."

As I have said, I have known Bob for over forty years. That is because he is my father and I cannot begin to tell you how many times I have heard the above quote growing up. If it were not in person, then it was on the airwaves as his signature sign-off of his radio shows. It was even made real and tangible for me when I was in grade school. I cannot remember the occasion or exact year, but my dad had given to me a specially autographed Wilson football. The kind with three regular textured brown panels and one stark-white panel. Inscribed on it was the above quote prefaced with how proud he was of me at that particular time, for no particular reason. However, this pigskin was signed, "Love Dr. Daddy".

For a young boy, as simple as it was, it was one of the best gifts ever. More importantly, I had known and grew up with the quote; and although millions heard it every time he cleared up the *Quiet Storm*, it took on a more personal note because he wasn't just Doctor Bob Lee, radio personality, to me he was Dr. Daddy!

This particular saying made me feel as if I was given a special gift for which a debt was owed. In conjunction with this particular quote another sums up my feelings in reference perfectly. "**To whom much is given, much is required.**"

My father has oft spoken of finding "your passion" or a driving motivator, as he has in reaching the masses through radio communications and education, and let that steer your life's course. Mine has always been physical activity and fittingly enough, education. To date, I have been an educator for 15 years, ranging from the public school to the charter school to the international school sectors and have taught every grade level from Pre-Kinder to twelfth grade, as well as having held numerous leadership positions.

"Stay in school, study hard and stay out of trouble!" Growing up, education has always had a prominent place within the family and if you ask any aunt, uncle or cousin what the most spoken quote in the family would be and who said it, hands down the above quote would be attributed to "Daddy" or Grampa John.

This second Lee family quote was stressed so often that many in our family eventually went into education as professionals or have incorporated some sort of educational aspect within their careers or daily lives. While we take pride in all of our extended family members, we can boast of having Professors, Instructors, Educational

Introduction

Administrators and NGO administrators among our ranks. Additionally, we are continuous learners. One of my sisters is an R.N. and is currently exploring a masters in Acute Nurse Practitioner or in Education. This year, I even find myself back in school, as well, pursuing my masters in Educational Leadership.

If you know my father, you know that he did not put this book together hastily without forethought or research or out of hubris. It was conceived and developed to educate and provoke thought. To enlighten the reader on the insights and critical thoughts of some of humanity's greatest thinkers. I end this passage by advising you, the reader, to enjoy this book in any number of ways. Read it from cover to cover if you choose. Or perhaps, browse the contents page and skip around to sections that draw you in. No matter which way you finally decide, I am positive that you will find more than one quote, whether they are often used, familiar or newly discovered, that resonates within you. Either way, I trust that you will keep this book in a handy spot for quick reference.

Finally, I leave you with these last quotes that I am fond of and try to weave into my everyday life. They hold every bit as much significance today, as when they were initially spoken and both are attributed to Socrates. One of those aforementioned great thinkers I wrote of, teacher of Plato, and considered to be the father of western philosophy.

The first espouses, **"There is only one good, knowledge, and one evil, ignorance."**

The last simply states, **"The only true wisdom is in knowing you know nothing."**

- Shiheim Wilson Lee

Your Daily Dose of Quotes and Anecdotes

"You never know where your blessings will come from; sometimes they happen so fast, and you've always got to be ready."

- Doctor Bob Lee

INTRODUCTION

My purpose in writing this book is to help you *Make the Grade*. As a matter of fact, I have been thinking about writing it for more than a decade, but I finally decided to put pen to paper.

I consider myself a "wordsmith" because I am fascinated by words, I understand, remember and use them well. But my main claim to fame is that I specialize in identifying with the people in the community by accessing or translating their "lingo" and responding in kind. Much of what I have been blessed with comes from my ability to mentally retain the dialogue that I have heard throughout my life. I can recall many times when my Grandparents, Parents, Teachers, Aunts, Uncles, Ministers, Coaches or Neighbors might have said something to me as a life's lesson that stuck in my mind. With just a few simply stated words of wisdom from someone who cared, I really do believe that my life took many turns away from trouble and instead led me toward triumph.

After testing the waters, I eventually found my calling as an on-air radio personality. A key element to my success is listening, dissecting, remembering and repeating words that are meaningful. I listen to what is being stated, absorb it and respond to it spontaneously - hundreds of thousands of words each day crossing the airwaves to and from hundreds of thousands of people each week.

The words I hear from my various audiences don't always make sense, they're not always proper or good words and they occasionally create a challenge for me; but I have learned to respond to them spontaneously, without hesitation and repeat them only as I see fit. I always try to think before I speak and thus, choose my words wisely.

Because of my commitment to serve the community, I have put together more than a thousand of my favorite quotes and anecdotes - some are from famous people and some are from not so famous people. But, in my opinion, if you read, understand, and apply the words within these pages, many of them can and will make a difference in your life. I sifted through thousands of "words of wisdom" and have compiled what I consider to be a diverse and meaningful selection of quotes, which can:

- Show you many meaningful lessons to improve your life
- Enlighten you up so you can gain knowledge
- Feed your spirit, so you can feel good about yourself
- Help you step into every day as a more confident and happier person

The dialogue has come in the form of Quotes and Anecdotes, many of which I have decided to share with you because of the positive messages that they relay. As you read through the pages, make notes. You might find answers to many of your questions about life, living, surviving, and succeeding.

My selection of **Quotes and Anecdotes** has touched upon many subjects, including Make the Grade Foundation's Seven Principles: Parents, Teachers, Students, Community, Spirituality, Health and Financial Literacy. Plus, beyond those seven principles, I have touched on: Love, Forgiveness, Friendship, Acceptance, Motivation, Inspiration and Success. I hope my choices will help all of you – the sons and daughters, the parents and grandparents of those sons and daughters – journey towards triumph. Read the words within, become inspired, think about what they mean, and if they are fitting, act upon them.

"Never give up on something you can't go a day without thinking about."
- Sir Winston Churchill

PART ONE

SEVEN MOTIVATING PRINCIPLES

Parents, Teachers, Students, Community, Spirituality, Health and Financial Literacy

Your Daily Dose of Quotes and Anecdotes

I think that a caring family, friends and neighbors are some of the things that are missing today – some of the things that would keep young people in line.

- Bob Lee

ONE

PARENTS

Now that I am a father and a grandfather I often reflect about my own childhood to determine what principles taught to me and what words repeated to me had the most influence over my life. When I look back on those days, I realize how important it was for my father to repeat this particular message over and over: "Stay in school, study hard and stay out of trouble!"

My father continued to stress the importance of love, family and education. He repeated his messages often so that my brothers and sisters and I could have a bright future. He knew that it could only take one mistake to destroy our lives.

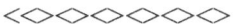

I think parents need to communicate more with their children and try to understand their concerns. Get together on a daily basis and sit side by side with your children to help them with their homework. As a parent, you should always know who your children are hanging out with. So, instead of just dropping them off at school and treating school like it is a babysitting service, you should go to your children's school and find out what's going on there, make friends with the teachers, keep in contact with the guidance counselor and principal and get to know who you need to know and everything that's going on in the school. Volunteer – make yourself visible!

Debrah Harris-Johnson is no stranger to volunteering. The mother of two is a professional mediator who focuses her energy on helping youth make the transition to adulthood a little easier. She is the author of *The African American Teenage Guide to Personal Growth, Health, Safety, Sex and Survival* (Amber Books). In her book, Debrah said this about the relationships between teens and their parents:

> Healthy and constructive parent-child interactions (should) lead to warm and loving relationships. This, in turn, promotes the development of happier, more confident, and more secure children. In short, mutually rewarding family relationships are not just accidents. They are the result of positive interactions between parents and their children. However, the reverse is also true. Repeated parent-child interactions filled with scolding, tension, accusations, and unpredictable emotional outbursts can strain even the best of relationships. Parents should instead take a moment or two to think about how much their children mean to them and how good their child can make them feel. They make you laugh; they make you proud…they care what you think, what you say, what you do, and how you are feeling. They love you, trust you and miss you when you are gone. They probably come to you for just about everything…it's gratifying to be loved and needed like that. It's great to be a parent!"

It is so important for parents to assume the responsibility of their children. But, that is not always possible. Given the ills of our society and the climate of most inner-city communities, there are far too many kids who are cheated out of the experience of living in a two-parent home. When these children are not being cared for properly or being abused, their life and the lives of those around them could be in danger. Acting like an adult does not always fall into the hands of grown people; sometimes young people must step up and report wrong-doings to those in authority. We must all make a commitment to protect our youth through outreach and concern, whenever the need arises.

When your children are in the adolescent stage, don't just throw your hands in the air and give up when they start acting up. The key, as parents or guardians, is to continue to give our youngsters all the tools necessary to help them become successful. That includes taking them on trips, giving them classes, interacting with their teachers, attending their extracurricular activities, and more. With all these incentives in place, parents and guardians will certainly help their children to be successful in life.

Asadah Kirkland is an award-winning author whose first published book, *Beating Black Kids* is designed to encourage better actions amongst her parental peers and should help parents and all adults make better decisions concerning children. According to Ms. Kirkland:

> "A child's contribution to the world does not have to come hard. Struggle does not have to be involved. There is nothing wrong with things being easier for them. Easier feels good and has great value if we have the skill as adults to create it.
>
> Our children will populate the world in the future, as adults. There is no denying that. *What kind of adults will they be? As parents, we influence the answer. Will we put them in a corner or give them the opportunity to decide on something? Will they remember our beatings or will they remember our wisdom?"*

Regardless of the family structure you are raising your children in; it is up to you as a parent or "foster" parent to keep your children safe from harm. Always find time to listen to your children, no matter what their age, so they have the best possible chance of growing up as upstanding and responsible citizens. And remember, honesty is the best policy. If you are facing problems, find a way to share them with your children and let them know they can always share their problems with you – no matter how small or how big they are. Being honest can save a life.

According to actress Irene Cara: "There are a lot of things that help you succeed, but above everything it takes belief in yourself. More than anything else, have confidence. There are a lot of people out there who will put you down; but the way to win is to put your trust in your ability because you will need that. I had to overcome a couple of things: being a Latina and the fact that I did not come from money. A lot of my peers, at the time, were sons and daughters of well-off parents. My parents were very giving, loving and always encouraging me, so I never felt disadvantaged, even though in a lot of ways we were. As a parent, it's important to encourage your children and give them the proper support."

Taiki Matsuura stated: "I've found that many loving parents have lost focus of what parenting is about. Our obligation as parents is not to make our children happy – it's to teach them how to be happy; it's not to make our children comfortable – it's to teach them how to tolerate discomfort. For these lessons, upsetting to them as they may be now, will better equip them for survival later when it matters most."

Parents need to see that every situation that their kids find themselves in is a teaching situation, and they need to take the time to explore cost and effect. So, talking to your children, explaining things to children as to why things happen in the world. Getting them to see cost and relationships between events is the best way to increase comprehension skills.

BOB'S 123 FAVORITE QUOTES ABOUT THE PARENT

1. ". . . I would have let him go one finger at a time, until, without his realizing, he'd be floating without me. And then I thought, perhaps that is what it means to be a [parent] - to teach your child to live without you." - **Nicole Krauss**

2. "Our children are only as brilliant as we allow them to be." - **Eric Micha'el Leventhal**

3. Your children need your presence more than your presents." - **Jesse Jackson**

4. "It takes 20 years to build a reputation and five minutes to ruin it." - **Warren Buffett**

5. "You can have everything in life you want, if you will just help other people get what they want." - **Zig Ziglar**

6. "The time is always right to do what is right." - **Martin Luther King, Jr.**

7. "If we do not discipline ourselves the world will do it for us." - **William Feather**

8. "The whole secret of a successful life is to find out what is one's destiny to do, and then do it." - **Henry Ford**

9. "You don't choose your family. They are God's gift to you, as you are to them." - **Desmond Tutu**

10. "The struggle of today, is not altogether for today - it is for a vast future also." - **Abraham Lincoln**

11. "Worry not that your child listens to you; worry most that they watch you." - **Ronald A. Heifetz**

12. "Raising teenage sons and daughters is a long and tiresome journey. With God's help, the final outcome will be worthwhile." - **Ana Monnar**

13. "Happiness is when you realize that your kids have grown up to be AWESOME people!" - **Tanya Masse**

14. "Children are mirrors; they will always show you exactly what is going on inside of you. Each phase of their growth is an opportunity to heal your own pain, to go deeper inside yourself and become more truly human" - **Vimala McClure**

15. "Nobody works harder at learning than a curious kid." - **Thomas L. Friedman**

16. "No one said parenting was easy, but NO good parent has any right to give up. It is one labyrinth you can never quit because it seems too hard." - **Gillian Duce**

17. "All children think unkindly of their parents at some time or another." - **Kenneth MacKenzie**

18. "The goal of a true family is not that their children follow in their footsteps, but that their children surpass them in all ways." - **Andrew Vachss**

19. "Dust is the parent of a star!" - **Munia Khan**

20. "Your children are going through life with their eyes closed, so YOU'RE the one who has to steer." - **Jennifer Senior**

21. "A good example is the best gift you can offer to your children. In your absence, your example is present, which means you are present always!" - **Israelmore Ayivor**

22. "Train a child in the way he should go, and when he is old he will not depart from it." - **Bible**

23. "Being a parent is like being a catcher. You gotta handle whatever is thrown your way." - **Tom Swyers**

24. "It's certainly TOUGH being AWESOME all the time, but I do it so the kids have someone to look up to!" - **Tanya Masse**

25. "It takes a society to raise a generation." - **David Berman**

26. "Acknowledge and voice the positives LOUDER than the negatives." - **Tanya Masse**

49. "What's done to children, they will do to society." - **Karl Menninger**

50. "You have a lifetime to work, but children are only young once." - **Polish Proverb**

51. "My parents just tell me, if you know what you want, you should stay determined and go for it. You can do anything." - **Aaliyah**

52. "One of the things that my parents have taught me is never listen to other people's expectations. You should live your own life and live up to your own expectations, and those are the only things I really care about it." -**Tiger Woods**

53. "My heroes are and were my parents. I can't see having anyone else as my heroes." - **Michael Jordan**

54. "Every great dream begins with a dreamer. Always remember, you have within you the strength, the patience, and the passion to reach for the stars to change the world." - **Harriet Tubman**

55. "Never underestimate the power of dreams and the influence of the human spirit. We are all the same in this notion; the potential for greatness lives within each of us." - **Wilma Rudolph**

56. "The battles that count aren't the ones for gold medals. The struggles within yourself -The invisible, inevitable, battles inside all of us-that's where it's at." – **Jesse Owens**

57. "I have a dream that my four little children will one day live in a nation where they will not be judged by the color of their skin, but by the content of their character." - **Dr. Martin Luther King Jr.**

58. "We cannot always build the future for our youth, but we can build our youth for the future." - **Franklin D. Roosevelt**

59. "Parenthood...It's about guiding the next generation, and forgiving the last." - **Peter Krause**

60. "It is time for parents to teach young people early on that in diversity there is beauty and there is strength. We all should know that diversity makes for a rich tapestry, and we must understand that all the threads of that tapestry are equal in value no matter their color." - **Maya Angelou**

61. "Greatness occurs when your children love you, when your critics respect you and when you have peace of mind." - **Quincy Jones**

62. "In every conceivable manner, the family is link to our past, bridge to our future." - **Alex Haley**

63. "If we continually try to force a child to do what he is afraid to do, he will become more timid, and will use his brains and energy, not to explore the unknown, but to find ways to avoid the pressures we put on him. If, however, we are careful not to push a child beyond the limit of his courage, he is almost sure to get braver." - **John Holt**

64. "Never do for a child what he is capable of doing for himself." – **Elizabeth Hainstock**

65. "Whatever you would have your children become, strive to exhibit in your own lives and conversation." - **Lydia H. Sigourney**

66. "If a child is to keep alive his inborn sense of wonder without any such gift from the fairies, he needs the companionship of at least one adult who can share it, rediscovering with him the joy, excitement and mystery of the world we live in." - **Rachel Carson**

67. "The last step in parental love involves the release of the beloved; the willing cutting of the cord that would otherwise keep the child in a state of emotional dependence." - **Lewis Mumford**

68. "Children thrive when parents set before them increasingly difficult, but always meetable challenges." - **Anonymous**

69. "Call them rules or call them limits, good ones, I believe, have this in common: they serve reasonable purposes; they are practical and within a child's capability; they are consistent; and they are an expression of loving concern." - **Fred Rogers**

70. "I think that the best thing we can do for our children is to allow them to do things for themselves, allow them to be strong, allow them to experience life on their own terms, allow them to take the subway... let them be better people, let them believe more in themselves." - **C. Joy Bell**

71. "The best way to keep children at home is to make the home atmosphere pleasant, and let the air out of the tires." - **Dorothy Parker**

72. "You know your children are growing up when they stop asking you where they came from and refuse to tell you where they're going." - **P.J. O'Rourke**

73. "Our children are only as brilliant as we allow them to be." - **Eric Micha'el Leventhal**

74. "A single action can cause a life to veer off in a direction it was never meant to go. Falling in love can do that, you think. And so can a wild party. You marvel at the way each has the power to forever alter an individual's compass. And it is the knowing that such a thing can so easily happen, as you did not know before, not really, that has fundamentally changed you and your son." - **Anita Shreve**

75. "Having kids - the responsibility of rearing good, kind, ethical, responsible human beings - is the biggest job anyone can embark on. As with any risk, you have to take a leap of faith and ask lots of wonderful people for their help and guidance. I thank God every day for giving me the opportunity to parent." - **Maria Shriver**

76. "There are times when parenthood seems nothing more than feeding the hand that bites you." - **Peter De Vries**

77. "It wasn't until we dropped him at his university dormitory and left him there looking touchingly lost and bewildered amid an assortment of cardboard boxes and suitcases in a spartan room not unlike a prison cell that it really hit home that he was vanishing out of our lives and into his own." - **Bill Bryson**

78. "It's not so much that I mind listening to her stories. Everybody likes to have an audience - that's why most people have kids, isn't it?" - **Robin Epstein**

79. "When we raise our children to Shine, the future becomes brighter!" - **Brigette Foresman**

80. "Passing their toilet training is the very last thing that some adults did that has made their parents proud of them." - **Mokokoma Mokhonoana**

81. "A man can make a son but a true man would be a father. A lady can have a child, but a real mother raises the child." - **Sofia Reyes**

82. "Taking good care of your husband or wife is the best way to thank their parent or parents for having taken good care of them." - **Mokokoma Mokhonoana**

83. "To receive children's love and to come home to a child who runs to you with a hug, among the most powerful emotional experiences available." - **Dennis Prager**

84. "Black people love their children with a kind of obsession. You are all we have, and you come to us endangered." - **Ta-Nehisi Coates**

85. "If my children think I'm genuine, no one else's opinion matters to me." - **Beth Moore**

86. "It is the most miserable thing to feel ashamed at home." - **Charles Dickens**

87. "The more you care, the more you fear." - **Wayne Gerard Trotman**

88. "Our ferocious commitment to our children's safety and success, along with our genuine love, drives us to endure the often unhappy experience of disciplining our children." - **Matt Chandler**

89. "I believe my mother was smart enough to know that in the night, you are willing to tell all. If she waited until the next day, she knew she'd get one-syllable answers." - **H.W. Brands**

90. "When you take your place as the authority figure in your home, your child will feel more safe in the real world, not the screen world." - **Gary Chapman**

91. "Millions of deaths would not have happened if it weren't for the consumption of alcohol. The same can be said about millions of births." - **Mokokoma Mokhonoana**

92. "Parents who are afraid to put their foot down usually have children who step on their toes." - **Chinese Proverb**

93. "Even very young children need to be informed about dying. Explain the concept of death very carefully to your child. This will make threatening him with it much more effective." - **P. J. O'Rourke**

94. "By the time a man realizes that maybe his father was right, he usually has a son who thinks he's wrong." - **Charles Wadsworth**

95. "Raising kids is part joy and part guerilla warfare." - **Ed Asner**

96. "If we as parents listen, we can give children what they need based on who they are and what they want for themselves." - **Asadah**

97. "Listening to parents' advice is sort of like watching commercials. You know what's coming, you've heard it all before, it's a big bore, but you listen anyway." - **Author Unknown**

98. "Making the decision to have a child is momentous. It is to decide forever to have your heart go walking around outside your body." - **Elizabeth Stone**

99. "Let the children show what they know and let the world sing their praises." - **Asadah**

100. "Always kiss your children goodnight - even if they're already asleep." - **H. Jackson Brown, Jr.**

101. "It kills you to see them grow up. But I guess it would kill you quicker if they didn't." **- Barbara Kingsolver**

102. "Parents often talk about the younger generation as if they didn't have anything to do with it." - **Dr. Haim Ginott**

103. "Parents wonder why the streams are bitter, when they themselves have poisoned the fountain." - **John Locke**

104. "Parents have become so convinced that educators know what is best for their children that they forget that they themselves are really the experts."
 - **Marian Wright Edelman**

105. "Children desperately need to know - and to hear in ways they understand and remember - that they're loved and valued by mom and dad." - **Paul Smally**

106. "An infallible way to make your child miserable is to satisfy all his demands." - **Henry Home**

107. "Some parents could do more for their children by not doing so much for them." - **Author Unknown**

108. "Parents who are always giving their children nothing but the best usually wind up with nothing but the worst." - **Author Unknown**

109. "One of the greatest titles in the world is parent, and one of the biggest blessings in the world is to have parents to call mom and dad." - **Jim DeMint**

110. "The parents exist to teach the child, but also they must learn what the child has to teach them; and the child has a very great deal to teach them." - **Arnold Bennett**

111. "To understand your parents' love, you must raise children yourself." - **Chinese Proverb**

112. "Do not educate your child to be rich. Educate them to be happy. So, when they grow up, they'll know the value of things, not the price." - **Unknown**

113. "I believe that we parents must encourage our children to become educated, so they can get into a good college that we cannot afford." - **Dave Barry**

114. "I think if we are actually going to accept our generation's responsibility, that's going to mean that we give our children no less retirement security than we inherited from our parents." - **Carol Moseley Braun**

115. "Every home is a university and the parents are the teachers." - **Mahatma Gandhi**

116. "Believe it or not, the worst thing to hear from your parents is 'I'm Disappointed in you." - **Unknown**

117. "Family is the first school for young children, and parents are powerful models." - **Alice Sterling Honig**

118. "Have you ever noticed how parents can go from the most wonderful people in the world to totally embarrassing in three seconds?" - **Rick Riordan**

119. "When I was a kid my parents moved a lot, but I always found them." - **Rodney Dangerfield**

120. "By loving them for more than their abilities we show our children that they are much more than the sum of their accomplishments." - **Eileen Kennedy-Moore**

121. "Parents aren't the people you come from. They're the people you want to be, when you grow up." - **Jodi Picoult**

122. "When I was a boy, I passed a homeless man, drunk and begging on a street corner. My father, sensing my disgust, said something I never forgot, that I think of every time I see your face on the news or in the paper- "That man was once someone's little boy." - **Blake Crouch**

123. "A little girl and her father were crossing a bridge. The father was kind of scared so he asked his little daughter: "Sweetheart, please hold my hand so that you don't fall into the river." The little girl said: "No, Dad. You hold my hand." "What's the difference?" Asked the puzzled father. "There's a big difference," replied the little girl. "If I hold your hand and something happens to me, chances are that I may let your hand go. But if you hold my hand, I know for sure that no matter what happens, you will never let my hand go." In any relationship, the essence of trust is not in its bind, but in its bond. So, hold the hand of the person whom you love rather than expecting them to hold yours..." - **Unknown**

SUMMARY: The Parent

The Bible sums up the role of a parent in a proverb which reads, "Train up a child in the way he should go: Even when he is old he will not depart from it." (Proverbs 22:6)

The job of a parent is the job of a trainer. Wisely prepare your child to honor God, parents, and those around them, and you have done well.

Because of the dedication and commitment of the thousands of teachers throughout the country, our youth have an opportunity to build a meaningful future. Education, however, is but one component that must go into our commitment to give our youth the best possible platform for their successful future.

By being well-educated, our youth will not have any guarantees, but they will at least become a more confident and more competitive society in the job market when the time comes for them to step out on their own.

According to **Ewon Foster**, Educator and Author of *The Game Plays You*, "When you have on the armor of education, you are not only affording yourself power and opportunity, you are also declaring that you have what it takes to make the cut and you will "go hard" for your place in this world. People who know your story will respect you for taking control of your destiny and not allowing your difficult beginnings to dictate the outcome of your life. You will be an asset to your community, which will inspire others who are going through a similar situation and feel they have no way out. Be the one to show them how it's done!"

If you define your purpose, learn from your mistakes and find great role models, your journey toward success will be a lot easier. I firmly believe that the best way to succeed starts with a good education. Mix in some hard work, dedication and determination and by helping yourself you will have the tools to help others.

BOB'S 100 FAVORITE QUOTES ABOUT THE TEACHER

1. "The good teacher makes the poor student good and the good student superior". - **Anonymous**

2. "Those who educate children well are more to be honored than they who produce them; for these only gave them life, those the art of living well." - **Aristotle**

3. "They inspire you, they entertain you, and you end up learning a ton even when you don't know it" - **Nicholas Sparks**

4. "I am indebted to my father for living, but to my teacher for living well." - **Alexander the Great**

5. "A teacher who loves learning earns the right and the ability to help others learn." - **Ruth Beechick**

6. "A mind is a terrible thing to waste."
   - **the United Negro College Fund**

7. "We have an obligation and a responsibility to be investing in our students and our schools. We must make sure that people, who have the grades, the desire and the will, but not the money, can still get the best education possible."
   - **President Barack Obama**

8. "When teachers doubt your potential, show them how wrong they truly are." - **Ace Antonio Hall**

9. "When you have on the armor of education, you are not only affording yourself power and opportunity, but you are also declaring that you have what it takes to make the grade."
   – **Doctor Bob Lee**

10. "I spent half my childhood trying to be like my dad. True for most boys, I think. It turns with adolescence. The last thing I wanted was to be like my dad. It took becoming a man to realize how lucky I'd been. It took a few hard knocks in life to make me realize the only thing my dad had ever wanted or worked for was to give me a chance at being better than him." - **Tucker Elliot**

11. "If an education does not teach the person how to live right, then the fact is that it is also not teaching how to make the right living." - **Anuj Somany**

12. "AWESOME TEACHERS recognize different abilities, take time to listen, go beyond the textbooks, and inspire from the heart!" - **Tanya Masse**

13. "The ultimate purpose of a teacher is to teach students to think in a better way." - **Debasish Mridha, M.D.**

14. "Education is unfolding the wings of head and heart together. The job of a teacher is to push the students out of the nest to strengthen their wings." - **Amit Ray**

15. "Sometimes, the experts forget they were once beginners. You must be gentle with beginners; they have great potential to be experts." - **Lailah Gifty Akita**

16. "In the 21st century, one of the best anti-poverty programs is a world-class education." - **President Barack Obama**

17. "You can't learn anything from a person who knows everything." - **Marty Rubin**

18. "A genuine teacher does not seek to impress you with their greatness, but instead to impress upon you that you possess the skills to discover your own." - **Charles F. Glassman**

19. "You can find anyone that will tell you what you want to hear, but the only one worth valuing is the one that tells you what you need to learn." - **Shannon L. Alder**

20. "Don't just leave your footprints in the sand only to be washed away as the ocean waves come crashing to the shore. You want to impact the lives of others in such a way that you'll be remembered forever. You want to instill values and wisdom in the hearts and minds of others that will never be forgotten. So, they may teach their children to carry on from generation to generation." - **Amaka Imani Nkosazana**

21. "At its highest level, the purpose of teaching is not to teach—it is to inspire the desire for learning. Once a student's mind is set on fire, it will find a way to provide its own fuel." - **Sydney J. Harris**

22. "Great teachers have high expectations for their students, but even higher expectations for themselves." - **Todd Whitaker**

23. "The point of being a teacher is to do more than impart facts, it's to shape the way students perceive the world, to help a student absorb the rules of a discipline. The teachers who do that get remembered." - **David Brooks**

24. "To teach, learn. To learn, teach." - **Mokokoma Mokhonoana**

25. "For my success, I am immensely grateful to God, my parents, my family, my friends, my teachers and to the books I read." - **Amit Kalantri**

26. "That's what teaching is, the art of explanation: presenting the right information in the right order in a memorable way." - **Taylor Mali**

27. "A kid shouldn't need a diagnosis to access help." - **Ross W. Greene**

28. "Regard mistakes as teachers, not judges!" - **Tae Yun Kim**

29. "Good teachers are priceless. They inspire you, they entertain you, and you end up learning a ton even when you don't know it." - **Nicholas Sparks**

30. "Great teachers will never be able to make up for bad parents, nor should they be expected to." - **Taylor Mali**

31. "The best teachers become the best teachers by being their own best students." - **Laurie Gray**

32. "A teacher is a compass that activates the magnets of curiosity, knowledge, and wisdom in the pupils." - **Ever Garrison**

33. "I cannot teach anybody anything, I can only make them think." - **Socrates**

34. "If you are planning for a year, sow rice; if you are planning for a decade, plant trees; if you are planning for a lifetime, educate people." - **Chinese Proverb**

35. "Education breeds confidence. Confidence breeds hope. Hope breeds peace." - **Confucius**

36. "Every child deserves a champion – an adult who will never give up on them, who understands the power of connection and insists that they become the best that they can possibly be." - **Rita Pierson**

37. "If someone is going down the wrong road, he doesn't need motivation to speed him up. What he needs is education to turn him around." - **Jim Rohn**

38. "Tell me and I forget. Teach me and I remember. Involve me and I learn." - **Benjamin Franklin**

39. "A mind when stretched by a new idea never regains its original dimensions." - **Anonymous**

40. "The best way to predict your future is to create it." - **Abraham Lincoln**

41. "Education is not filling of a pail but the lighting of a fire." - **William Butler Yeats**

42. "The function of education is to teach one to think intensively and to think critically. Intelligence plus character – that is the goal of true education." - **Martin Luther King, Jr.**

43. "Children must be taught how to think, not what to think." - **Margaret Mead**

44. "Teaching is more than imparting knowledge, it is inspiring change. Learning is more than absorbing facts, it is acquiring understanding." - **William Arthur Ward**

45. "Education is what survives when what has been learned has been forgotten." - **B.F. Skinner**

46. "When you learn, teach. When you get, give."
    - **Maya Angelou**

47. "Don't just teach your kids to read, teach them to question what they read. Teach them to question everything!" - **George Carlin**

48. "I am not a teacher, but an awakener." - **Robert Frost**

49. "A child miseducated is a child lost." - **John F. Kennedy**

50. "Live as if you were to die tomorrow. Learn as if you were to live forever." - **Mahatma Gandhi**

51. "What we learn with pleasure we never forget."
    -**Alfred Mercier**

52. "The beautiful thing about learning is that no one can take it away from you." - **B.B. King**

53. "Logic will get you from A to B. Imagination will take you everywhere." - **Albert Einstein**

54. "The hardest thing to teach is how to care." - **Unknown**

55. "Education is the most powerful weapon which you can use to change the world." - **Nelson Mandela**

56. "A teacher affects eternity; he can never tell where his influence stops." - **Henry Adams**

57. "Laughter is timeless. Imagination has no age. And dreams are forever." -**Walt Disney**

58. "Each of us has a fire in our hearts for something. It's our goal in life to find it and keep it lit." - **Mary Lou Retton**

59. "Plant your own garden and decorate your own soul, instead of waiting for someone to bring you flowers."
    - **Veronica A. Shoffstall**

The Teacher

60. "Without education, your children can never really meet the challenges they will face. So, it's very important to give children education and explain that they should play a role for their country**." - Nelson Mandela**

61. "The more that you read, the more things you will know, the more that you learn, the more places you'll go."
    -Mahatma Ghandi

62. "Around here, we don't look backwards for very long… We keep moving forward, opening up new doors and doing new things because we're curious… and curiosity keeps leading us down new paths." **- Walt Disney**

63. "You can teach a student a lesson for a day; but if you can teach him to learn by creating curiosity he will continue the learning process as long as he lives." **- Clay P. Bedford**

64. "Do not confine your children to your own learning, for they were born in another time." **- Chinese Proverb**

65. "Have the proper attitude. Stay in school. Have the ability to appreciate things and say *Thank you* when the need arises." - **Congressman Ed Towns**

66. "Know what you have, know what you want and know the quality of people you surround yourself with. No matter where you come from, you should prioritize your brain power." **- Kris Aman**

67. "A little learning, indeed, may be a dangerous thing, but the want of learning is a calamity to any people."
    - Frederick Douglass

68. "Any book that helps a child to form a habit of reading, to make reading one of his deep and continuing needs, is good for him." **- Maya Angelou**

69. "Books were my pass to personal freedom. I learned to read at age three, and soon discovered there was a whole world to conquer that went beyond our farm in Mississippi."
    - Oprah Winfrey

70. "Education helps one cease being intimidated by strange situations." - **Maya Angelou**

71. "Education is a precondition to survival in America today." -**Marian Wright Edelman**

72. "Education is all a matter of building bridges." -**Ralph Ellison**

73. "Education is for improving the lives of others and for leaving your community and world better than you found it." - **Marian Wright Edelman**

74. "Education is the key to unlock the golden door of freedom." - **George Washington Carver**

75. "EDUCATION is the medium by which a people are prepared for the creation of their own particular civilization, and the advancement and glory of their own race." - **Marcus Garvey**

76. "Education is the passport to the future, for tomorrow belongs to those who prepare for it today." -**Malcolm X**

77. "From the first, I made my learning, what little it was, useful every way I could." - **Mary McLeod Bethune**

78. "I have often reflected upon the new vistas that reading opened to me. I knew right there in prison that reading had changed forever the course of my life. As I see it today, the ability to read awoke in me some long dormant craving to be mentally alive." - **Malcolm X**

79. "If they took the idea that they could escape poverty through education, I think it would make a more basic and long-lasting change in the way things happen. What we need are positive, realistic goals and the willingness to work. Hard work and practical goals." - **Kareem Abdul-Jabbar**

80. "It is hard to apply oneself to study when there is no money to pay for food and lodging. I almost never explain these things when folks are asking me why I don't do this or that."
 - Zora Neale Hurston

81. "It is not who you attend school with but who controls the school you attend." **- Nikki Giovanni**

82. "My Alma mater was books, a good library... I could spend the rest of my life reading, just satisfying my curiosity."
 - Malcolm X

83. "My mother said I must always be intolerant of ignorance but understanding of illiteracy. That some people, unable to go to school, were more educated and more intelligent than college professors." **- Maya Angelou**

84. "The strong spirit empowers others to be stronger souls."
 - Lailah Gifty Akita

85. "The educational system of a country is worthless unless it [revolutionizes the social order]. Men of scholarship, and prophetic insight, must show us the right way and lead us into light which is shining brighter and brighter."
 - Carter G. Woodson

86. "The greatest education in the world is watching the masters at work." **- Michael Jackson**

87. The masses make the nation and the race. If the masses are illiterate, that is the judgment passed on the race by those who are critical of its existence." **- Marcus Garvey**

88. "The whole world opened to me when I learned to read."
 – Mary McLeod Bethune

89. "Too often the educational value of doing well what is done, however little, is overlooked. One thing well done prepares the mind to do the next thing better. Not how much, but how well, should be the motto. One problem thoroughly understood is of more value than a score poorly mastered."
 - Booker T. Washington

90. "When bright young minds can't afford college, America pays the price." - **Arthur Ashe**

91. "Without education, you are not going anywhere in this world." -**Malcolm X**

92. "Through perseverance many people win success out of what seemed destined to be certain failure." - **Benjamin Disraeli**

93. "The quality of a person's life is in direct proportion to their commitment to Excellence, regardless of their chosen field of endeavor." - **Vince Lombardi**

94. "What is defeat? Nothing but education, Nothing but the first step to something better." - **Wendell Phillips**

95. "Let us remember: One book, one pen, one child, and one teacher can change the world." - **Malala Yousafzai**

96. "I think education is power. I think that being able to communicate with people is power. One of my main goals on the planet is to encourage people to empower themselves." - **Oprah Winfrey**

97. "The dream begins with a teacher who believes in you, who tugs and pushes and   leads you to the next plateau, sometimes poking you with a sharp stick called *truth*."   - **Dan Rather**

98. "Like the sun, a teacher enlightens a mind with his love, warmth, and light." - **Debasish Mridha**

99. "A good teacher can inspire hope, ignite the imagination, and instill a love of learning." - **Brad Henry**

100.   "We must never forget our teachers, our lecturers and our mentors, who in their individual capacities have contributed to our academic, professional and personal development."   - **Lailah Gifty Akita**

SUMMARY: The Teacher

The job of a teacher is more significant than most think. The Bible gives sound counsel to teachers, saying: "Teach them his decrees and instructions, and show them the way they are to live and how they are to behave." (Exodus 18:20)

At a mere glance, you can see this teaching role is bigger than classrooms. Parents, mentors, and others must play a role in teaching young people.

Yes, We Can!

– Barack Obama

THREE

THE STUDENT

Barack Obama was a good student, not necessarily a "model student", but he always aspired to be better. Focusing on his studies rather than on his circumstances, Barack Obama navigated through the challenges of his youth and into the main arena as one of the most powerful men in the world.

As a young teenager, many of my encounters involved bullying incidents that stemmed from aggressive behavior from either older students or other young people around my age.

My environment and genetic circumstances may have been the cause of some of the incidents that I encountered, but once I met some positive adult role models, I became more confident about who I was and who I could become. As I began to get my bearings as a young adult, I realized that I wanted to help students, who like myself, needed something or someone to impact their decision.

I strongly recommend that you seek personal fulfillment by making sure you get involved in a career path that you really enjoy doing because you're going to have to work for the rest of your life. Here is what I have come to realize, particularly in this age of technology:

> *The adolescent stage is very tough – it's a tough part of growing up because many of the kids feel sort of in the dark. Young people today spend a lot of alone time and thus there is very little comradeship, teamwork, bonding or loyalty. However, it's important, if you're going to hang out with a*

group of people, make sure you are all leaders, and make sure everybody knows right from wrong.

Much of the breakdown between kids and their parents occurs when 'tweens and teens begin to lose respect for them and begin to rely on their peers for all the answers, right or wrong. Younger students are still moldable; you can really get into their minds and teach them.

I believe that every adult who is in a position to help young people learn to become more knowledgeable and successful students should take this responsibility upon themselves whenever possible. First and foremost, we must teach young people to step up to the plate and not just stay in one place and think everything will come to them.

Journalist and International Film Critic, Kam Williams stated: "When I was graduating from grammar school, my father wrote a quote from Shakespeare's Hamlet in my yearbook, which has stuck with me forever. It was Polonius' advice to his son Laertes: "This above all to thine own self be true." These wise words served me well as a constant reminder to keep my eye on the lofty academic and spiritual standards I'd set for myself in life, and they especially came in handy at those moments when I was tempted to fall prey to the instant gratification offered by superficial, material pursuits."

As the founder and director of Make the Grade Foundation, I wanted to teach kids to identify their purpose. I let them know that when I was young, I didn't know exactly what I wanted to do; but that I eventually identified something in my life that I loved doing. My broadcasting career started as a hobby, but I enjoyed it so much that it became my full-time profession. In fact, when they first started paying me for the work that I'm doing I told them, *you've got to be kidding me because I used to do this for free.* I said *you guys are paying me for what I really love doing? I love this!*"

You don't want to be employed on a job and not loving it, so make sure you embark on a career path that you really enjoy because you're going to have to work somewhere for the rest of your life.

Sometimes, your focus is so wide that you don't know exactly what to do. When you begin to narrow down that focus, it shows. Here's a personal illustration: When I used to box, I played football and participated in other sports, as well. I also deejayed and got involved in music; and I even learned about and got involved in the printing business. But it wasn't until I narrowed it all down that I began to flourish in the one or two things that I really loved doing.

If you pinpoint something that you're truly passionate about, God will give you thousands of ideas to help support your passion. You may even come up with some exceptional ideas that, possibly some new discoveries or inventions, because God is backing you up and giving you the knowledge to complete the task. It may seem like an easy plan but don't take anything for granted; even professional athletes and famous entertainers must practice many hours in solitude to make their jobs look "easy." They create a mindset of self-discipline to match their passion. That's what successful people do…focus. Stay on the straight and narrow, study hard, set your goal, and go for it. You may encounter a few pitfalls along the way, but don't let that discourage you; your determination can keep you on course.

I didn't realize it until years later, but upon reflecting, the preparation for my college education probably began as early as when I was in diapers. By the time I was in high school, I was at a good point to prepare for and succeed in college. One of the best ways to prepare for college is to understand what classes to take while you are in high school. And of course, keep going for A's and take classes that stimulate and challenge you.

Despite your special interests, though, the following classes are *musts* for all aspiring college students! The better your grades in these classes, the better your chances for college admission and financial aid assistance.

- ❖ 4 years of English
- ❖ 4 years of math (meaning courses that begin with algebra)
- ❖ 2-3 years of history
- ❖ 3-4 years of a foreign language
- ❖ 2-3 years of science

When you begin your junior year at high school you should be clear about where you will be attending college – in state or out of state. However, you may not yet have made a final decision about the college you will be attending. The best thing to do is keep attending college fairs in your area. These events are the next best thing to visiting every school. Then you should narrow the application process to a minimum of three colleges and be aware of their deadlines!

11-time drag racing champion, **Ricky Gadson** stated, "I tell kids to go to school, reach for the moon and at least you'll land among the stars. I am the winning professional drag racer, a 9-time world champion and I've always had my own drag racing team. I've been doing this for 27 years and I was the first African American to break through the color barrier. It took a lot for me because people kept writing in to see what was going on, but I kept winning. It was hard in the beginning – I didn't have anyone – my father died when I was five – my mother also died when I was young. When I was 18, I decided to give it a year. In 1998, I was in the right place at the right time when I became the first and only African American to win…and I am still the only one. When I was going to school, I didn't have a dream to be a racer. I have been told that it's important to be diverse and not put all my eggs in one basket; so, I also have a trucking company and a drag racing school."

As a high school student, I did not yet have a clear path about my journey or where I was going; but I am sure that God had already given me a purpose; I just needed to identify it. Little did I know, I was just a few years away from embarking upon that clear path.

Doctor Arnette F. Crocker stated, "Our ancestors were right on point when they said, "It takes a village to raise a child. In order to effectively educate a child, it demands a multidimensional approach. It requires thinking outside of the status quo, meeting the needs of the students, and empowering them to find their purpose in life. We must help our young people to establish goals and assist them in developing a plan, which will support them in reaching their highest potential. It is crucial that young people understand that "making the grade" is not just about what they achieve today, it is more about how "making the grade" will ultimately impact their tomorrow."

As my professional career evolved, I became a community leader with the establishment of Make the Grade Foundation. In an effort to involve high school students in something that would attract their interest, New York radio personality Ken Webb and I went to one of the local high schools and asked the students, "Hey you guys like the Internet, right?" They all said, *Yah!* Then I said, "How would you like to do Internet radio? They said, *"How does it work?"* I told them, "You're gonna say something and I am gonna teach you how to program it so you can broadcast it." Those kids really got into it.

Mentoring students is a good thing. I challenge my peers to live by the philosophy of "Each One Teach One." At one time, we were all students; but what matters most is "what kind of student you become." I had great mentors along the way. With their encouragement, I remained steadfast and became a good student. By passing my baton

The Student

to new students, I am confident that the career paths of many generations to come have become clearer.

Doctor Roscoe C. Brown, Jr. shared his journey toward success: "I come from a generation of African-Americans where we were always trying to be better. My father, Dr. Roscoe C Brown, Sr, was an official in the United States Public Health Service. I went to the Dunbar High School in Washington, DC, the most competitive high school in the country for blacks. In addition to our academic work, we were very competitive athletically. I was one of the first blacks to play lacrosse. I also played football and basketball. Just as my parents kept my interest peaked and talked to me about new activities, we need to talk to young people about how "It's Cool to Be Smart." We were taught to be very competitive in order to succeed throughout life. When I was a young child my parents took me to see the Spirit of St. Louis hanging from the ceiling of the Smithsonian, in Washington, DC and that got me interested in aviation. Then I began to make models of airplanes, and I would fly them with rubber bands. When World War II started, the military began an experimental group that was to be trained in Tuskegee, Alabama. They went to colleges and recruited the best leaders and athletes to be Tuskegee Airmen. At the time, I was in my junior year at Springfield College in Springfield, Massachusetts, where I was valedictorian of my class. Because they had R.O.T.C. when I was in high school, I had already earned a commission as an infantry officer when I was 18-years-old. I resigned my commission, signed up to be a Tuskegee Airman, did my training in Tuskegee, and then got my wings in 1944. I did my combat training in Walterboro, South Carolina, went overseas, and flew combat until the war ended."

Captain Roscoe Brown commanded the 100th Fighter Squadron of the 332nd Fighter Group, known as the Tuskegee Airmen, during World War II. He flew 68 long-range missions from August of 1944 to March of 1945. He is credited with being the first 15th Air Force pilot to shoot down a German jet fighter, a feat that happened on March 24,

1945 while escorting bombers near Berlin. It was the longest escort mission to take place in the war.

Dr. Brown earned multiple awards for his actions in WWII including: The Distinguished Flying Cross and the Air Medal with eight Oak Leaf Clusters. In 2000, he was among those in attendance when President George W. Bush presented the Tuskegee Airmen the Congressional Gold Medal. During an interview, Dr. Brown asserted: "We defeated a stereotype that African-Americans didn't have the intelligence, the ability to do this. And we did it, we did it as well, many times better than other folks..."

After leaving the Air Force Dr. Brown followed his passion to teach and embarked upon a long career in education. He was the Director of the Center for Urban Education Policy and University Professor at the Graduate School and University Center of The City University of New York (CUNY). He was also the past President of Bronx Community College of CUNY, and former Director of the Institute of Afro-American Affairs at New York University.

As his student and his friend, I learned a lot from Dr. Brown. He was a true hero, not only for his leadership as a Tuskegee Airman but for his mentorship to the countless young people who were fortunate to learn from him and from the organizations that he directed. He was a Founding Board member and served as a Founding an Advisory Board Member for Make the Grade Foundation until he passed away July 2, 2016 at the age of 94.

BOB'S 100 FAVORITE QUOTES FOR THE STUDENT

1. "The world is a severe schoolmaster, for its frowns are less dangerous than its smiles and flatteries, and it is a difficult task to keep in the path of wisdom." - **Phillis Wheatley**

2. "I really don't think life is about the I-could-have-beens. Life is only about the I-tried-to-do. I don't mind the failure but I can't imagine that I'd forgive myself if I didn't try."
   - **Nikki Giovanni**

3. "If you're walking down the right path and you're willing to keep walking, eventually you'll make progress."
   - **Barack Obama**

4. "How far you go in life depends on your being tender with the young, compassionate with the aged, sympathetic with the striving, and tolerant of the weak and strong. Because someday in your life you will have been all of these."
   - **George Washington Carver**

5. "Living in the moment means letting go of the past and not waiting for the future. It means living your life consciously, aware that each moment you breathe is a gift."
   - **Oprah Winfrey**

6. "There are people in your life whom you unknowingly inspire simply by being you." - **Unknown**

7. "Have a vision. Be demanding." - **Colin Powell**

8. "If I am walking with two other men, each of them will serve as my teacher. I will pick out the good points of the one and imitate them, and the bad points of the other and correct them in myself." - **Confucius**

9. "In a world filled with hate, we must still dare to hope. In a world filled with anger, we must still dare to comfort. In a world filled with despair, we must still dare to dream. And in a world filled with distrust, we must still dare to believe."
   – **Michael Jackson**

10. "It's not the load that breaks you down, it's the way you carry it." – **Lena Horne**

11. "You learn far more from negative leadership than from positive leadership. Because you learn how not to do it. And, therefore, you learn how to do it." - **Norman Schwarzkopf**

12. "Our nation is a rainbow – red, yellow, brown, black, and white – and we're all precious in God's sight."
    - **Jesse Jackson**

13. "Never be limited by other people's limited imaginations. If you adopt their attitudes, then the possibility won't exist because you'll have already shut it out…You can hear other people's wisdom, but you've got to re-evaluate the world for yourself." – **Mae Jemison**

14. "You're not to be so blind with patriotism that you can't face reality. Wrong is wrong, no matter who does it or says it."
    – **Malcolm X**

15. The outside world told black kids when I was growing up that we weren't worth anything. But our parents said it wasn't so, and our churches and our schoolteachers said it wasn't so. They believed in us, and we, therefore, believed in ourselves."
    – **Marian Wright Edelman**

16. "I have come to believe over and over again that what is most important to me must be spoken, made verbal and shared, even at the risk of having it bruised or misunderstood."
    – **Audre Lorde**

17. "You're not obligated to win. You're obligated to keep trying to do the best you can every day."
    – **Marian Wright Edelman**

18. "No one should negotiate their dreams. Dreams must be free to flee and fly high. No government, no legislature, has a right to limit your dreams. You should never agree to surrender your dreams." – **Jesse Jackson**

19. "Hate is too great a burden to bear. It injures the hater more than it injures the hated." – **Coretta Scott King**

20. "If you don't like something, change it. If you can't change it, change your attitude." – **Maya Angelou**

21. "Change will not come if we wait for some other person or some other time. We are the ones we've been waiting for. We are the change that we seek." – **Barack Obama**

22. "One of the lessons that I grew up with was to always stay true to yourself and never let what somebody else says distract you from your goals. And so, when I hear about negative and false attacks, I really don't invest any energy in them, because I know who I am." – **Michelle Obama**

23. "Two things are infinite: the universe and human stupidity; and I'm not sure about the universe." – **Albert Einstein**

24. "I have fallen in love with the imagination. And if you fall in love with the imagination, you understand that it is a free spirit. It will go anywhere, and it can do anything."
    - **Alice Walker**

25. "A room without books is like a body without a soul."
    – **Marcus Tullius Cicero**

26. "Don't cry because it's over, smile because it happened."
    – **Dr. Seuss**

27. "Me doing the right thing has absolutely nothing to do with you doing the right thing." – **Jack Lash**

28. "If you want to have a life that is worth living, a life that expresses your deepest feelings and emotions and cares and dreams, you have to fight for it." - **Alice Walker**

29. "Don't wait, the time will never be just right."
    – **Napoleon Hill**

30. "The meaning of life is to find your gift. The purpose of life is to give it away." – **Anonymous**

31. "Opportunities don't happen, you create them."
    – **Chris Grosse**

32. "It is not because things are difficult that we do not dare; it is because we do not dare that they are difficult." – **Red Jacket**

33. "I do not know anyone who has got to the top without hard work; that is the recipe. It will not always get you to the top; but should get you pretty near." – **Margaret Thatcher**

34. "That some achieve great success is proof to all that others can achieve it as well." – **Abraham Lincoln**

35. "Courage is like a muscle; we strengthen it by use."
    – **Ruth Gordon**

36. "It takes nothing to join a crowd; it takes everything to stand alone." – **Hans F Hansen**

37. "I believe that every right implies a responsibility, every opportunity an obligation, every possession a duty."
    – **John D. Rockefeller**

38. "To be prepared for war is one of the most effective means of preserving peace." – **George Washington**

39. "Through perseverance many people win success out of what seemed destined to be certain failure." – **Benjamin Disraeli**

40. "People pay attention to people who participate."
    – **Councilman Andy King**

41. "When obstacles arise, you change your direction; to reach your goal, you do not change your decision to get there."
    – **Zig Ziglar**

42. "I've been absolutely terrified every moment of my life and I've never let it keep me from doing a single thing that I wanted to do." – **Georgia O'Keeffe**

43. "Without courage wisdom bears no fruit."
    – **Baltasar Gracian**

44. "If you want to play a game, go to where it's played and find a way to get in; things happen when you get in the game." – **Chris Matthews**

45. "Someone is sitting in the shade today because someone planted a tree a long time ago." – **Warren Buffett**

46. Success is not final, failure is not fatal: it is the courage to continue that counts." – **Winston Churchill**

47. "The probability that we may fail in the struggle ought not to deter us from the support of a cause we believe to be just." – **Abraham Lincoln**

48. "You can never cross the ocean until you have the courage to lose sight of the shore." – **Christopher Columbus**

49. "Thinking is the hardest work there is, which is probably the reason why so few engage in it." – **Henry Ford**

50. "Years from now you will be more disappointed by the things that you didn't do than by the ones you did do." – **Mark Twain**

51. "I have not failed. I've just found 10,000 ways that won't work." – **Thomas Edison**

52. "A pessimist sees the difficulty in every opportunity, an optimist sees the opportunity in every difficulty." – **Winston Churchill**

53. "Only when the tide goes out do you discover who's been swimming naked." – **Warren Buffett**

54. "Obstacles are those frightful things you see when you take your eyes off your goal." – **Henry Ford**

55. Success consists of going from failure to failure without loss of enthusiasm." – **Winston Churchill**

56. "There seems to be some perverse human characteristic that likes to make easy things difficult." – **Warren Buffett**

57. "When everything seems to be going against you, remember that the airplane takes off against the wind, not with it." – **Henry Ford**

58. "Life is like riding a bicycle. To keep your balance, you must keep moving." – **Albert Einstein**

59. "I can accept failure, everyone fails at something. But I can't accept not trying." – **Michael Jordan**

60. "You don't learn to walk by following rules. You learn by doing, and by falling over." – **Richard Branson**

61. "The secret of getting ahead is getting started." – **Mark Twain**

62. "Formal education will make you a living; self-education will make you a fortune." – **Jim Rohn**

63. "Life consists not in holding good cards but in playing those you hold well." – **Josh Billings**

64. "Better to do something imperfectly than to do nothing perfectly." – **Robert Schuller**

65. "Your attitude, not your aptitude, will determine your altitude." – **Zig Ziglar**

66. "Success is nothing more than a few simple disciplines, practiced every day." – **Jim Rohn**

67. "Success seems to be largely a matter of hanging on after others have let go." – **William Feather**

68. A successful man is one who can lay a firm foundation with the bricks others have thrown at him." – **David Brinkley**

69. "If you tell the truth, you don't have to remember anything." – **Mark Twain**

70. "Motivation is what gets you started. Habit is what keeps you going." – **Jim Rohn**

71. "If you aim at nothing, you will hit it every time." – **Zig Ziglar**

72. "Numerous politicians have seized absolute power and muzzled the press. Never in history has the press seized absolute power and muzzled the politicians."
    – **David Brinkley**

73. "The absence of alternatives clears the mind marvelously."
    – **Henry Kissinger**

74. "We must accept finite disappointment, but never lose infinite hope." – **Martin Luther King, Jr.**

75. "Do not bring people in your life who weigh you down. And trust your instincts ... good relationships feel good. They feel right. They don't hurt. They're not painful. That's not just with somebody you want to marry, but it's with the friends that you choose. It's with the people you surround yourselves with." – **Michelle Obama**

76. "Be like a postage stamp. Stick to one thing until you get there." – **Josh Billings**

77. "Tough times never last, tough people do."
    – **Robert Schuller**

78. "Many of life's failures are people who did not realize how close they were to success when they gave up."
    – **Mark Twain**

79. "This is my time. You understand me? It doesn't matter what you tried to do. You couldn't destroy me. I'm still standing. I'm still strong and I always will be."
    – **-Antoine Fisher**

80. "The unsuccessful person is burdened by learning, and prefers to walk down familiar paths. Their distaste for learning stunts their growth and limits their influence."
    – **John C. Maxwell**

81. "A diamond is a chunk of coal made good under pressure."
    – **Henry Kissinger**

82. "One way to get the most out of life is to look upon it as an adventure." – **William Feather**

83. "A wise man can learn more from a foolish question than a fool can learn from a wise answer." – **Bruce Lee**

84. "Opportunity is missed by most people because it is dressed in overalls and looks like work." – **Mark Twain**

85. "Success is no accident. It is hard work, perseverance, learning, studying, sacrifice and most of all, love of what you are doing or learning to do." – **Pele**

86. "You can't play sports without losing sometimes and, in losing, you learn something about grace and how to act under pressure." – **John F. Kerry**

87. "I'd rather attempt to do something great and fail than to attempt to do nothing and succeed." – **Robert Schuller**

88. "Blessed is he who has learned to admire but not envy, to follow but not imitate, to praise but not flatter, and to lead but not manipulate." – **William Arthur Ward**

89. "The task of the leader is to get his people from where they are to where they have not been." – **Henry Kissinger**

90. "No one is born hating another person because of the color of his skin, or his background, or his religion. People must learn to hate, and if they can learn to hate, they can be taught to love, for love comes more naturally to the human heart than its opposite." – **Nelson Mandela**

91. "The world is a dangerous place to live; not because of the people who are evil, but because of the people who don't do anything about it." – **Albert Einstein**

92. "I've failed over and over and over again in my life. And that is why I succeed." – **Michael Jordan**

93. "If we did all the things we are capable of, we would literally astound ourselves." – **Mark Twain**

94. "The best students come from homes where education is revered: where there are books, and children see their parents reading them." – **Leo Buscaglia**

95. "Students rarely disappoint teachers who assure them in advance that they are doomed to failure." – **Sidney Hook**

96. "Our laws guarantee all students the right to a K-12 education, regardless of their immigration status."
  – **Wendy Kopp**

97. "Students achieving Oneness will move on to Twoness."
  – **Woody Allen**

98. "I would suggest that teachers show their students concrete examples of the negative effects of the actions that gangsta rappers glorify." – **Kareem Abdul-Jabbar**

99. "I believe that everyone has a story, and it is important that we encourage all students to tell theirs." – **Erin Gruwell**

100. "I tell my students there is such a thing as writer's block and they should respect it. It's blocked because it ought to be blocked because you haven't got it right now."
  – **Toni Morrison**

SUMMARY: The Student

The Bible discusses carefully the relationship between the student and teacher. In yesteryear, parents would carefully select who was going to pour into their child because of this Bible verse: "The student is not above the teacher, but everyone who is fully trained will be like their teacher." (Luke 6:40)

Think wisely about who teaches your children, and examine the teacher's life as well. When you find a good teacher, the student must then submit and learn well.

All men are caught in an inescapable network of mutuality, tied in a single Garment of destiny. Whatever affects one directly affects all indirectly. I can never be what I ought to be until you are what you ought to be, and you can never be what you ought to be until I am what I ought to be.

- Martin Luther King, Jr.

FOUR

THE COMMUNITY

Sometimes when you feel like you're not doing enough, you should reach out to the community to give back. It's very important for people in our community to look out for our youngsters—to protect the community. All these things worked hand-in-hand while I was growing up and it was a great support system.

In addition to my father, I was blessed to have Hank Carter as a coach and mentor during my youth. He was like another parent in the community who looked out for all of us kids. and he instilled in me the discipline to take on the necessary actions to become successful. Hank also taught me about giving back and looking out for people in need. I was lucky that our paths crossed. His encouragement to always give back to the Community, was one of the many facets in my life that inspired me to establish an organization which would raise awareness and uplift the young people that I encountered.

For more than 20 years, I had visited numerous organizations and schools throughout the Tri-State area, mentoring Youth and families. Not knowing quite what it would be, I prayed and meditated. Through the calmness and quiet, I visualized an organization that could tie all the necessary entities together. My goal with founding the Make the

Grade Foundation was to restore the sense of community that is missing in today's society.

John Elmore, Esq., author of **The African American Criminal Justice Guide** stated, "It hurts me to see so many of our young men going to jail instead of college. Many go to jail, having been wrongfully convicted of crimes that they did not commit. Others will go to jail because of a lack of economic opportunities; and others go to jail simply because they did not have someone to show them."

If you know that your family is struggling financially or from domestic issues, don't waste time wondering why or wallowing in self-pity, anger or pain. It's always good, no matter what your age, to find someone – a responsible teen role model or a mentoring adult or organization that you can talk to about your problems at home. The advice and concern that you may get could ultimately save your life… don't be afraid to ask. But, by all means, steer clear from other troubled youth who will probably lead you down the wrong path to resolve your problems. It sounds like it could be a lot of responsibility for a kid; but I remember when I had to choose my company carefully and it wasn't always easy.

As my life stabilized and I learned the value of being responsible for my own actions, I recognized the importance of establishing an organization that would offer guidance to young people who may not be able to figure it all out the way I did. For many reasons, they may not have been fortunate to have parents who care or role models who were readily available to them. So, I decided to show kids that there are alternative ways to having a more productive life and a brighter future.

I think it's very important for the people in our community to look out for our youngsters. In a community that shows concern for all who live there, that positive environment can eventually overrule the negative aspects and help to cultivate and protect the children.

Lily Yeh, global artist and founder of the Rwanda Healing Project stated: "When I see brokenness, poverty and crime in inner cities, I also see the enormous potential and readiness for transformation and rebirth. We are creating an art form that comes from the heart and reflects the pain and sorrow of people's lives. It also expresses joy, beauty, and love. This process lays the foundation of building a genuine community in which people are reconnected with their families, sustained by meaningful work, nurtured by the care of each other and will together raise and educate their children. Then we witness social change in action."

At Make the Grade Foundation we inspire young people by focusing on a collaboration between parent, teacher, student, community, and spirituality. In addition, we offer a financial literacy component; and in order to help the young people learn better, we have stressed the health component in regard to healthy eating as well as healthy living…both physically and mentally. We discuss all those things that are useful to help youngsters become successful by guiding them in the right direction.

It is of great concern to me that, even when it comes to something like playing simple games like jacks, checkers and other board games, or dodge ball, hide and go seek, or jump rope, they don't experience the same quality of games that we used to play. Although games are important to round out your personality there is very little interaction or physical challenge because everything is so technical and only requires thumb coordination. Youth today spend a lot of alone time and thus there is very little comradeship, teamwork, bonding or loyalty. Make the Grade Foundation stresses the education factor first and foremost by offering a series of programs.

I am personally digging back, trying to help the kids do things the way they used to be done – by showing them the care and concern that I experienced from my parents, teachers, community and spirituality – when I was growing up.

BOB'S 100 FAVORITE QUOTES ABOUT COMMUNITY

1. "I am of the opinion that my life belongs to the whole community and as long as I live, it is my privilege to do for it whatever I can. I want to be thoroughly used up when I die, for the harder I work the more I live."
   – **George Bernard Shaw**

2. "Without a sense of caring, there can be no sense of community." – **Anthony Burgess**

3. "A community is like a ship; everyone ought to be prepared to take the helm." – **Henrik Ibsen**

4. "Community cannot for long feed on itself; it can only flourish with the coming of others from beyond, their unknown and undiscovered brothers." – **Howard Thurman**

5. "It is vain to talk of the interest of the community, without understanding what is the interest of the individual."
   – **Jeremy Bentham**

6. "A racially integrated community is a chronological term timed from the entrance of the first black family to the exit of the last white family." – **Saul Alinsky**

7. "While the spirit of neighborliness was important on the frontier because neighbors were so few, it is even more important now because our neighbors are so many."
   – **Lady Bird Johnson**

8. "It is not more bigness that should be our goal. We must attempt, rather, to bring people back to...the warmth of community, to the worth of individual effort and responsibility...and of individuals working together as a community, to better their lives and their children's future."
   – **Robert F. Kennedy**

9. "Each of us must rededicate ourselves to serving the common good. We are a community. Our individual Fates are linked; our futures intertwined; and if we act in that knowledge and in that spirit together, as the Bible says: "We can move mountains." – **Jimmy Carter**

10. "The golden way is to be friends with the world and to regard the whole human family as one." – **Mahatma Gandhi**

11. "But many of us seek community solely to escape the fear of being alone. Knowing how to be solitary is central to the art of loving. When we can be alone, we can be with others without using them as a means of escape." – **bell hooks**

12. "Many people are good at talking about what they are doing, but in fact do little. Others do a lot but don't talk about it; they are the ones who make a community live."

    – **Jean Vanier**

13. "Beauty is not who you are on the outside, it is the wisdom and time you gave away to save another struggling soul like you." – **Shannon L. Alder**

14. "One of the marvelous things about community is that it enables us to welcome and help people in a way we couldn't as individuals. When we pool our strength and share the work and responsibility, we can welcome many people, even those in deep distress, and perhaps help them find self-confidence and inner healing." – **Jean Vanier**

15. "To build community requires vigilant awareness of the work we must continually do to undermine all the socialization that leads us to behave in ways that perpetuate domination."

    – **Bell Hooks**

16. "A person with ubuntu is open and available to others, affirming of others, does not feel threatened that others are able and good, for he or she has a proper self-assurance that comes from knowing that he or she belongs in a greater whole and is

diminished when others are humiliated or diminished, when others are tortured or oppressed."
    – **Desmond Tutu**

17. "Every person is defined by the communities she belongs to." – **Orson Scott Card**

18. "A growing community must integrate three elements: a life of silent prayer, a life of service and above all of listening to the poor, and a community life through which all its members can grow in their own gift." – **Jean Vanier**

19. "Being considerate of others will take you and your children further in life than any college or professional degree."
    – **Marian Wright Edelman**

20. "Everybody can be great... because anybody can serve. You don't have to have a college degree to serve. You don't have to make your subject and verb agree to serve. You only need a heart full of grace. A soul generated by love."
    – **Martin Luther King, Jr.**

21. "From what we get, we can make a living; what we give, however, makes a life." – **Arthur Ashe**

22. "I don't think you ever stop giving. I really don't. I think it's an on-going process. And it's not just about being able to write a check. It's being able to touch somebody's life."
    – **Oprah Winfrey**

23. "I'm profoundly changed. There's a bittersweet emotion that I feel from playing this role... I want the world to be different because I was here. However lofty or crazy or delusional that may sound, I want people's lives to be better because I was here." – **Will Smith**

24. "It's so clear that you have to cherish everyone. I think that's what I get from these older black women, that every soul is to be cherished, that every flower Is to bloom." – **Alice Walker**

25. "Service is the rent we pay to be living. It is the very purpose of life and not something you do in your spare time."
– **Marian Wright Edelman**

26. "The highest test of the civilization of any race is in its willingness to extend a helping hand to the less fortunate."
– **Booker T. Washington**

27. "First it is necessary to stand on your own two feet. But the minute a man finds himself in that position, the next thing he should do is reach out his arms." – **Kristin Hunter**

28. "There is always something to do. There are hungry people to feed, naked people to clothe, sick people to comfort and make well. And while I don't expect you to save the world I do think it's not asking too much for you to love those with whom you sleep, share the happiness of those whom you call friend, engage those among you who are visionary and remove from your life those who offer you depression, despair and disrespect." – **Nikki Giovanni**

29. "True heroism is remarkably sober, very undramatic. It is not the urge to surpass all others at whatever cost, but the urge to serve others at whatever cost." – **Arthur Ashe**

30. "What material success does is provide you with the ability to concentrate on other things that really matter. And that is being able to make a difference, not only in your own life, but in other people's lives." – **Oprah Winfrey**

31. "Each of us is a being in himself and a being in society, each of us needs to understand himself and understand others, take care of others and be taken care of himself."
– **Haniel Clark Long**

32. "Every individual has a place to fill in the world and is important in some respect whether he chooses to be so or not."
– **Nathaniel Hawthorne**

The Community

33. "Even if I knew that tomorrow the world would go to pieces I would still plant my apple tree." – **Dr. Martin Luther King Jr.**

34. "Obstacles don't have to stop you. If you run into a wall, don't turn around and give up. Figure out how to climb it, go through it, or work around it." – **Michael Jordan**

35. "Freedom is never given, it is won." – **A. Philip Randolph**

36. "You must never be fearful about what you are doing when it's right." – **Rosa Parks**

37. "The African race is a rubber ball. The harder you dash it to the ground, the higher it will rise." – **African Proverb**

38. "If you can't fly then run, if you can't run then walk, if you can't walk then crawl, but whatever you do keep moving forward." – **Dr. Martin Luther King Jr.**

39. "You're either part of the solution or part of the problem." – **(Leroy) Eldridge Cleaver**

40. "No race can prosper till it learns there is as much dignity in tilling a field as in writing a poem." – **Booker T. Washington**

41. "I have learned over the years that when one's mind is made up, this diminishes fear; knowing what must be done does away with fear." – **Rosa Parks**

42. "Never be limited by other people's limited imaginations." – **Dr. Mae Jemison**

43. "Laundry is the only thing that should be separated by color." – **unknown**

44. "Only in the darkness can you see the stars." – **Dr. Martin Luther King Jr.**

45. "I never thought of losing, but now that it's happened, the only thing is to do it right. That's my obligation to all the people who believe in me. We all have to take defeats in life." – **Muhammad Ali**

46. "We must be the change we wish to see."
   – **Mahatma Gandhi**

47. "The will to win, the desire to succeed, the urge to reach your full potential... these are the keys that will unlock the door to personal excellence." – **Confucius**

48. "The best way to find yourself is to lose yourself in the service of others." – **Mahatma Gandhi**

49. "We make a living by what we get, but we make a life by what we give." – **Winston Churchill**

50. "Only a life lived for others is a life worthwhile."
   – **Albert Einstein**

51. "I don't know what your destiny will be, but one thing I do know: the only ones among you who will be really happy are those who have sought and found how to serve."
   – **Albert Schweitzer**

52. "If you knew what I know about the power of giving, you would not let a single meal pass without sharing it in some way." – **Buddha**

53. "We are not put on this earth for ourselves, but are placed here for each other. If you are there always for others, then in time of need, someone will be there for you." – **Jeff Warner**

54. "He who wishes to secure the good of others, has already secured his own." – **Confucius**

55. "Caring has the gift of making the ordinary special."
   – **George R. Bach**

56. "Never doubt that a small group of thoughtful, committed citizens can change the world; indeed, it's the only thing that ever has." – **Margaret Mead**

57. "Love cannot remain by itself — it has no meaning. Love has to be put into action and that action is service."
   – **Mother Teresa**

58. "Everyone can be great, because everyone can serve."
– **Martin Luther King, Jr.**

59. "This country will not be a good place for any of us to live in unless we make it a good place for all of us to live in."
– **Theodore Roosevelt**

60. "I have found that among its other benefits, giving liberates the soul of the giver." – **Maya Angelou**

61. "The good we secure for ourselves is precarious and uncertain until it is secured for all of us and incorporated into our common life." – **Jane Addams**

62. "We can never get a re-creation of community and heal our society without giving our citizens a sense of belonging."
– **Patch Adams**

63. "In an age where community involvement and partnerships with civil society are increasingly being recognized as indispensable, there is clearly a growing potential for cooperative development and renewal worldwide."
– **Kofi Annan**

64. "A community is a group of people who have come together, and they work and they live to try and improve the standard of living and quality of life - and I don't mean money."
– **William Baldwin**

65. "We can begin by doing small things at the local level, like planting community gardens or looking out for our neighbors. That is how change takes place in living systems, not from above but from within, from many local actions occurring simultaneously." – **Grace Lee Boggs**

66. "Surplus wealth is a sacred trust which its possessor is bound to administer in his lifetime for the good of the community." – **Andrew Carnegie**

67. "We were born to unite with our fellow men, and to join in community with the human race." – **Cicero**

68. "Let's create an integrated global community where we have shared benefits and responsibilities, and we don't fight because of our differences." – **Bill Clinton**

69. "When we have inner peace, we can be at peace with those around us. When our community is in a state of peace, it can share that peace with neighboring communities."
– **The Dalai Lama**

70. "The challenge of social justice is to evoke a sense of community that we need to make our nation a better place, just as we make it a safer place."– **Marian Wright Edelman**

71. "For a community to be whole and healthy, it must be based on people's love and concern for each other."
– **Millard Fuller**

72. "Average people and the average community can change the world. You can do it just based on common sense, determination, persistence and patience." – **Lois Gibbs**

73. "Every individual has a place to fill in the world and is important in some respect whether he chooses to be so or not."
– **Nathaniel Hawthorne**

74. "Without community service, we would not have a strong quality of life. It's important to the person who serves as well as the recipient. It's the way in which we ourselves grow and develop." – **Dorothy Height**

75. "The impersonal hand of government can never replace the helping hand of a neighbor." – **Hubert Humphrey**

76. "How do we create a harmonious society out of so many kinds of people? The key is tolerance -- the one value that is indispensable in creating community." – **Barbara Jordan**

77. "I also believe that it's almost impossible for people to change alone. We need to join with others who will push us in our thinking and challenge us to do things we didn't believe ourselves capable of." – **Frances Moore Lappé**

78. "If poverty is a disease that infects the entire community in the form of unemployment and violence, failing schools and broken homes, then we can't just treat those symptoms in isolation. We have to heal that entire community."
   – **Barack Obama**

79. "We don't accomplish anything in this world alone ... and whatever happens is the result of the whole tapestry of one's life and all the weavings of individual threads from one to another that creates something." – **Sandra Day O'Connor**

80. "In our hectic, fast-paced, consumer-driven society, it's common to feel overwhelmed, isolated and alone. Many are re-discovering the healing and empowering role that community can bring to our lives. The sense of belonging we feel when we make the time to take an active role in our communities can give us a deeper sense of meaning and purpose." – **Robert Alan Silverstein**

81. "I'm not a politician. I only want to help relieve the suffering in communities, and I want to help people see their community in each other." – **Russell Simmons**

82. "Men exist for the sake of one another. Teach them then or bear with them." – **Marcus Aurelius Antoninus**

83. "Community means strength that joins our strength to do the work that needs to be done. Arms to hold us when we falter. A circle of healing. A circle of friends. Someplace where we can be free." – **Starhawk**

84. "You shouldn't get to live in society and give nothing back. People complain about their taxes, yet they do nothing for the community." – **Kathleen Turner**

85. "The universal brotherhood of man is our most precious possession." – **Mark Twain**

86. "What should young people do with their lives today? Many things, obviously. But the most daring thing is to create stable communities in which the terrible disease of loneliness can be cured." – **Kurt Vonnegut, Jr.**

87. "Teaching kids how to feed themselves and how to live in a community responsibly is the center of an education."
    – **Alice Waters**

88. "The love of our neighbor in all its fullness simply means being able to say, "What are you going through?"
    – **Simone Weil**

89. "There is no power for change greater than a community discovering what it cares about." – **Margaret J. Wheatley**

90. "A man is called selfish not for pursuing his own good, but for neglecting his neighbor's." – **Richard Whately**

91. "Despair shows us the limit of our imagination. Imaginations shared create collaboration, collaboration creates community, and community inspires social change."
    – **Terry Tempest Williams**

92. "An activist's job is to make public civil rights issues until there can be a climate for change." – **Reverend Al Sharpton**

93. "Blessed are those who can give without remembering and take without forgetting." – **Anonymous**

94. "It is not our differences that divide us. It is our inability to recognize, accept, and celebrate those differences."
    – **Audre Lorde**

95. "Unity is strength, division is weakness." – **Swahili proverb**

96. "Sticks in a bundle are unbreakable." – **Bondei proverb**

97. "Cross the river in a crowd and the crocodile won't eat you." – **African proverb**

98. "Many hands make light work." – **Haya (Tanzania) proverb**

99. "A single stick may smoke, but it will not burn."
    – **African proverb**

100. "If you want to go quickly, go alone. If you want to go far, go together." – **African proverb**

SUMMARY: The Community

The Bible teaches us to be in community. Hebrews 10:24-25 says: "And let us consider how to stir up one another to love and good works, not neglecting to meet together, as is the habit of some, but encourage one another."

People are molded and shaped in community, not isolation. Be in a community that motivates you to be better. This is why real estate in one community is more expensive than another: because good neighbors encourage you to do better. It is worth the investment to surround yourself with good community.

Faith is the first factor in a life devoted to service. Without it, nothing is possible. With it, nothing is impossible.

-Mary McLeod Bethune

FIVE

SPIRITUALITY

I believe wholeheartedly that very few things will work without God in your life.

Without a doubt, the number seven has always had a significance in my life. I am one of seven children born to my mom, who had her first child at the age of seventeen.

When I published my first book "7 Ways to Make the Grade: A Living Guide to Your Community's Success," I didn't realize that after more than two years of writing, packaging and preparation, the publishing date would turn out to be October 7th.

While completing the manuscript for my second book "Doctor Bob Lee Presents His 1200 Favorite Quotes and Anecdotes," I had no idea that it would be finalized during the seventh month (July) of 2017.

The Significance of the Number 7 in the Bible

Seven is the number of completeness and perfection (both physical and spiritual). It derives much of its meaning from being tied directly to God's creation of all things. According to Jewish tradition, the creation of Adam occurred on October 7th, 3761 B.C. (or the first day of Tishri, which is the seventh month on the Hebrew calendar). The word 'created' is used 7 times, while describing God's creative work (Genesis 1:1, 21, 27 three times; 2:3; 2:4). There are 7 days in a week and God's Sabbath is on the 7th day.

Spirituality

The Bible, as a whole, was originally divided into 7 major divisions. They are 1) the Law; 2) the Prophets; 3) the Writings, or Psalms; 4) the Gospels and Acts; 5) the General Epistles; 6) the Epistles of Paul; and 7) the book of Revelation. The total number of originally inspired books was forty-nine, or 7 x 7, demonstrating the absolute perfection of the Word of God.

Appearances of the Number Seven

There are at least seven men in the Old Testament who are specifically mentioned as a man of God. They are Moses (Joshua 14:6), David (2 Chronicles 8:14), Samuel (1Samuel 9:6, 14), Shemaiah (1Kings 12:22), Elijah (1 Kings 17:18), Elisha (2 Kings 5:8) and Igdaliah (Jeremiah 35:4).

In the book of Hebrews, written by the apostle Paul, he uses seven titles to refer to Christ. The titles are 'Heir of all things' (Hebrews 1:2), 'Captain of our salvation' (2:10), 'Apostle' (3:1), 'Author of salvation' (5:9), 'Forerunner' (6:20), 'High Priest' (10:21) and the 'Author and finisher of our faith' (12:2).

In Matthew 13 Jesus is quoted as giving seven parables (Matthew 13:3 - 9, 24 - 30, 31 - 32, 33, 44, 45 - 46, 47).

Seven Psalms are ascribed to David in the New Testament (Psalm 2, 16, 32, 41, 69, 95 and 109).

In the book of Revelation there are seven churches, seven angels to the seven churches, seven seals, seven trumpet plagues, seven thunders and the seven last plagues.

The first resurrection of the dead takes place at the 7th trumpet, completing salvation for the Church.

Number Seven is Linked with God's Annual Feast Days

There are 7 annual Holy Days, beginning with Passover and ending with the Last Great Day (the day after the Feast of Tabernacles ends in the fall). The cycle of the holy days is completed in 3 festival seasons by the 7th month of the sacred calendar: Passover and Unleavened Bread, 1st month; Pentecost, 3rd month; and Trumpets, Atonement, Tabernacles and Last Great Day, 7th month.

The Biblical Meaning of Number Seven

Jesus performed seven miracles on God's holy Sabbath Day (which ran from Friday sunset to Saturday sunset), thus affirming its continued sacredness to God and necessity in the life of the believer.

1. Jesus healed the withered hand of a man attending synagogue services (Matthew 12:9)
2. At a Capernaum synagogue, Jesus casts out an unclean spirit that possessed a man (Mark 1:21)
3. Right after the above miracle Jesus heals Peter's wife's mother of a fever (Mark 1:29)
4. A woman attending synagogue, who was made sick by a demon for eighteen years, is released from her bondage (Luke 13:11)
5. At a Pharisee's house eating a meal with the host and several lawyers, Jesus heals a man with dropsy (Luke 14:2)
6. A man who is disabled and unable to walk is healed at the pool of Bethesda (John 5:8 - 9)
7. Jesus heals a man born blind at the pool of Siloam (John 9:14)

Used 735 times (54 times in the book of Revelation alone), the number 7 is the foundation of God's word.

Realizing the spiritual value and significance of the Number 7 as it is applied to life, when I founded the Make the Grade Foundation, I incorporated 7 principles into the foundation's mission: Parents, Teachers, Students, Community, Spirituality, Health and Financial Literacy.

In an effort to help me bring Spiritual Meaning to the 7 Principles of the Make the Grade Foundation,

I reached out to a member of the clergy. Dimas Salaberrios is pastor of Infinity Bible Church in the South Bronx of New York City. An international speaker, Dimas is president of Concerts of Prayer Greater New York and holds a master of divinity degree from Alliance Theological Seminary. Pastor Dimas is also the author of *Street God: The Explosive True Story of a Former Drug Boss on the Run from the Hood--and the Courageous Mission That Drove Him Back.* I want to thank Pastor Dimas for responding to my request by offering his input about the significance of the Number 7 in the Bible in conjunction with the following scriptures:

The Parent
The Bible sums up the role of a parent in a proverb which reads, "Train up a child in the way he should go: Even when he is old he will not depart from it." (Proverbs 22:6)

The job of a parent is the job of a trainer. Wisely prepare your child to honor God, parents, and those around them, and you have done well.

The Teacher
The job of a teacher is more significant than most think. The Bible gives sound counsel to teachers, saying: "Teach them his decrees and instructions, and show them the way they are to live and how they are to behave." (Exodus 18:20)

At a mere glance, you can see this teaching role is bigger than classrooms. Parents, mentors, and others must play a role in teaching young people.

The Student
The Bible discusses carefully the relationship between the student and teacher. In yesteryear, parents would carefully select who was going to pour into their child because of this Bible verse: "The student is not

above the teacher, but everyone who is fully trained will be like their teacher." (Luke 6:40)

Think wisely about who teaches your children, and examine the teacher's life as well. When you find a good teacher, the student must then submit and learn well.

The Community
The Bible teaches us to be in community. Hebrews 10:24-25 says: "And let us consider how to stir up one another to love and good works, not neglecting to meet together, as is the habit of some, but encourage one another."

People are molded and shaped in community, not isolation. Be in a community that motivates you to be better. This is why real estate in one community is more expensive than another: because good neighbors encourage you to do better. It is worth the investment to surround yourself with good community.

Spirituality
Invest in your spiritual development. First Thessalonians 5:23 reminds us that we are made up of spirit, soul, and body, and we need to attend to all three. We must not be overly consumed with things in the natural realm. Romans 8:6 says, "For to be carnally minded is death, but to be spiritually minded is life and peace."

I recommend reading the Bible and spending lots of time in prayer to help your spirit mature.

Health
In order to experience a dynamic life, you must take care of your health. The Christian faith honors that. In Third John 1:2 it says: "Dear friend, I pray that you may enjoy good health and that all may go well with you, even as your soul is getting along well."

We must give attention to our physical condition.

Financial Literacy

It is critically important that you become a good steward of money. Financial literacy is the place to begin.

Avoid all shortcuts and "get rich quick" tactics. Proverbs 13:11 says, "Dishonest money dwindles away, but whoever gathers money little by little makes it grow." Make sure you learn to save, even little by little, and make financial literacy a topic of study.

Without a doubt, the absence of a religious upbringing unfailingly manifests itself in a person's character. During your childhood, every aspect of your life is shaped, including: your character, sense of responsibility, good and bad habits and your ability to cope with difficulties.

Young people need to know there's someone responsible for them being here on earth other than their mother and father. Above all, young people need to have faith and find out there is a God because that in itself can lay a moral and spiritual foundation in children.

◇◇◇◇◇◇

When I was a child, my parents instilled a strong sense of purpose in my life and they found it in their belief in God. As a youngster, I became grounded in the belief God would always be there for me, even when I'm at my lowest point possible and was taught that God doesn't give up on people, even when they make a mistake.

At this stage of my life, I do not dwell on what religion I am or what church I attend, but rather on the fact that I believe in and worship God.

Former diplomat, activist, pastor and Congressman from Georgia, Andrew Young stated: "You must pray. You can't allow yourself to get in the way of what God has intended for you. They don't want you to pray in school, but I think you must have a strong connection with God. You must have a good understanding that you can make it, but you have to do it through hard work and continuous efforts. Have confidence within yourself and faith in God."

Always remember this: what you are, is God's gift to you and what you make of yourself is your gift to God, so choose your choice, and let your choice control the choosing. God already gave your blessings to you, but you just have to activate them. Once you activate your blessings, anything is possible; you can go as far as you want to go, you'll become unstoppable.

God gave you two feet. Just put one in front of the other and step to what you need to do. I don't necessarily want to bring religion into public schools, but relating to what I feel is needed to make a child successful, I do want to make church a component in the schools.

T.D. Jakes shared, "I had no plan for success. Everything I had ever tried I failed at. But, then I realized when God begins to operate in your life, if you don't have a plan for success, you can abort the purpose of God because you're so used to fighting and struggling. Suppose you win? Are you prepared for the things you asked God for to come to pass? Can you handle the persecution and the jealousy that will come against you if your dreams come true? Can you handle the family members who will hate you because your dream happened? Are you ready for your vision to come to pass?"

If you pinpoint something that you're really passionate about, God will give you thousands of ideas to help support that. You may come up with ideas that are out of this world, possibly some new inventions, because God is backing you up and giving you the knowledge to complete the task. It sounds like an easy plan—focus and invest—but even professional athletes and famous entertainers must practice many hours in solitude to make their jobs look "easy." They create a mindset of self-discipline to match their passion. That's what successful people do. So, stay on the straight and narrow, study hard, set your goal, and go for it. You may encounter a few pitfalls along the way, but don't let that discourage you; your determination can keep you on course.

John's gospel contains seven "I am" statements made by Jesus. Their focus is on what happens after we become believers. When your faith and hope need a boost, connect to Jesus' beauty and power by reciting the 7 "Iams" and remembering what they mean:

1. THE BREAD OF LIFE

"I am the bread of life. He who comes to me will never go hungry, and he who believes in me will never be thirsty. (**John 6:35**)

2. THE LIGHT OF THE WORLD

"I am the light of the world. Whoever follows me will never walk in darkness, but will have the light of life." (**John 8:12**)

3. THE GATE

I am the gate; whoever enters through me will be saved. He will come in and go out, and find pasture. (**John 10:9**)

4. THE GOOD SHEPHERD

"I am the good shepherd. The good shepherd lays down his life for the sheep." (**John 10:11**)

5. THE RESURRECTION AND THE LIFE

"I am the resurrection and the life. He who believes in me will live, even though he dies; and whoever lives and believes in me will never die." (**John 11:25-26**)

6. THE WAY, THE TRUTH AND THE LIFE

"I am the way and the truth and the life. No one comes to the Father except through me." (**John 14:6**)

7. THE VINE

"I am the vine; you are the branches. If a man remains in me and I in him, he will bear much fruit; apart from me you can do nothing." (**John 15:5**)

BOB'S 100 FAVORITE QUOTES ABOUT SPIRITUALITY

1. "The religious community is essential, for alone our vision is too narrow to see all that must be seen. Together, our vision widens and strength is renewed." – **Mark Morrison-Reed**

2. "Faith is taking the first step even when you don't see the whole staircase." – **Martin Luther King, Jr.**

3. "God does not give people positions or jobs or good conditions such as they desire; they must do that for themselves. God does not build cities nor towns nor nations, nor homes, nor factories; men and people do that and all those who want must work for themselves and pray to God to give them strength to do it." – **Marcus Garvey**

4. "I believe in prayer. It's the best way we have to draw strength from heaven." – **Josephine Baker**

5. "I find it interesting that the meanest life, the poorest existence, is attributed to God's will, but as human beings become more affluent, as their living standard and style begins to ascend the material scale, God descends the scale of responsibility at commensurate speed." – **Maya Angelou**

6. "I go through the same problems all young people go through. Being in this business, I accept that there are positives and negatives but having a strong family base and a belief in God enables me to weather the storms." – **Aaliyah**

7. "I know that there is a God - the God within me that's always present and will protect me. I'm not afraid to climb any mountain, because I know that I'm protected. Even if I fall and die, I'm still protected. My faith is on that level."
    – **Halle Berry**

8. "I meditate and pray all the time. The faith and respect that I have in the power of God in my life is what I've used to keep myself grounded, and it has allowed me to move away from the storms that were in my life." – **Halle Berry**

9. "I never really look for anything. What God throws my way comes. I wake up in the morning and whichever way God turns my feet, I go." – **Pearl Bailey**

10. "If I were to say, "God, why me?" about the bad things, then I should have said, "God, why me?" about the good things that happened in my life." – **Arthur Ashe**

11. "It isn't until you come to a spiritual understanding of who you are - not necessarily a religious feeling, but deep down, the spirit within - that you can begin to take control." – **Oprah Winfrey**

12. "Throughout life people will make you mad, disrespect you and treat you bad. Let God deal with the things they do, cause hate in your heart will consume you too." – **Will Smith**

13. "Most of us wait until we're in trouble, and then we pray like the dickens. Wonder what would happen if, some morning, we'd wake up and say, "Anything I can do for You today, Lord?" – **Burton Hillis**

14. "People see God every day they just don't recognize him." – **Pearl Bailey**

15. "By following your dream, by believing in yourself and in God, you can and will find your purpose, and you will Succeed." – **Tony Rose**

16. "God's Word is your owner's manual for life. It contains principles for health, finance, marriage, other relationships, business, and much more." – **Rick Warren**

17. "God does not want us to do extraordinary things; He wants us to do ordinary things extraordinarily well." – **Bishop Gore**

18. "Mornings are considered the perfect time to pray. It is when you get a fresh start and just meditate on the goodness of God in your life." – **Rebecca Small**

19. "Even if we don't always know what is going on in our lives or things are changing, God knows and He has a plan to make things great for us." – **Patricia Meyers**

20. "When you keep your thoughts positive and focused on the possibilities, you are better able to find all the blessings that God wants you to have." – **Chris Johnston**

21. "When God puts love and compassion in your heart toward someone, He's offering you an opportunity to make a difference in that person's life." – **Joel Osteen**

22. "In other words, take the rubbish that life throws at you and turn it into something good with God's help." – **Olivia Hope**

23. "Though some of us have lived in families with varying degrees of dysfunction, God's design has always been that families will be people we can count on, who watch out for us no matter what." – **Dr. Stephen A. Gammon**

24. "When we finally see what God has called us to do, we can look back and realize that our past is the key to unlocking the 'door' to our purpose." – **E'yen A Gardner**

25. "When you feel lonely or as if people are despising you, prayers will help you stay calm and ensure you that no matter what God will never despise you and you are always his child."
– **Dr. Mary Lee**

26. "When we come to the end of our rope, that is where we find God." – **Adam Cumpston**

27. "One must be open to receiving God's Word and the enlightenment of the Holy Spirit. This is what it means to have 'ears to hear.'" – **Dan Delzell**

28. "God has promised that those who ask will receive, and that the door is to open to those that knock." – **Adrian Ryan Lyons**

29. "There are things that God does for us not because we deserve them, but because we are His children."
    – **Carol Nkambule**

30. "God is looking for people He can reveal His wisdom to."
    – **Brian Fleming**

31. "Live for today, but hold your hands open to tomorrow. Anticipate the future and its changes with joy. There is a seed of God's love in every event, every unpleasant situation in which you may find yourself." – **Barbara Johnson**

32. "Thank goodness, God has a sense of humor because I think that's why He has been so patient with me."
    – **Lindsey K. Rietzsch**

33. "Most people never become who they were meant to be purely because they are scared of falling. They always forget about God's hands waiting to catch them." – **Olivia Benjamin**

34. "Be the light to the world that God created you to be. Show the world Jesus' love in every action you take, and every word you speak." – **Nicole L Rivera**

35. "God allows us to experience the low points of life in order to teach us lessons that we could learn in no other way."
    – **C.S. Lewis**

36. "God created you for a purpose. Greatness is destined for your life." – **Carl Mathis**

37. "I write about the power of trying, because I want to be okay with failing. I write about generosity because I battle selfishness. I write about joy because I know sorrow. I write about faith because I almost lost mine, and I know what it is to be broken and in need of redemption. I write about gratitude because I am thankful - for all of it."
    – **Kristin Armstrong**

38. "Correct thy son, and he shall give thee rest; yea, he shall give delight unto thy soul." – **Bible (Proverbs 29. 17)**

39. "The child that never learns to obey his parents in the home will not obey God or man out of the home."
    – **Susanne Wesley**

40. "Children, obey your parents in the Lord; for this is right. Honor thy father and mother." – **Bible** (Ephesians 6.1)

41. "Parents are like God because you want to know they're out there and you want them to approve of your life, still you only call them when you're in a crisis and need something."
 – **Chuck Palahniuk**

42. "Let parents bequeath to their children not riches, but the spirit of reverence." – **Plato**

43. "To maintain a joyful family requires much from both the parents and the children. Each member of the family has to become, in a special way, the servant of the others."
 – **Pope John Paul II**

44. "If you raise your children to feel that they can accomplish any goal or task they decide upon, you will have succeeded as a parent and you will have given your children the greatest of all blessings." – **Brian Tracy**

45. "The spiritual life does not remove us from the world but leads us deeper into it." – **Henri J. M. Nouwen**

46. "The fact that I can plant a seed and it becomes a flower, share a bit of knowledge and it becomes another's, smile at someone and receive a smile in return, are to me continual spiritual exercises." – **Leo Buscaglia**

47. "Faith is the evidence of things not seen." – **Bible**

48. "If you can't have faith in what is held up to you for faith, you must find things to believe in yourself, for life without faith in something is too narrow a space to live."
 – **George Edward Woodberry**

49. "Believe in something larger than yourself." – **Barbara Bush**

50. "There is literally nothing that I ever asked to do, that I asked the blessed Creator to help me to do, that I have not been able to accomplish." – **George Washington Carver**

51. "All my life I have risen regularly at four o'clock and have gone into the woods and talked to God. There He gives me my orders for the day." – **George Washington Carver**

52. "We were born to make manifest the glory of God that is within us. It's not just in some of us, it's in everyone."
 – **Nelson Mandela**

53. "God answers all our prayers. Sometimes the answer is yes. Sometimes the answer is no. Sometimes the answer is, you've got to be kidding!" – **Jimmy Carter**

54. "I never went to bed in my life and I never ate a meal in my life without saying a prayer. I know my prayers have been answered thousands of times, and I know that I never said a prayer in my life without something good coming of it."
 – **Jack Dempsey**

55. "The essential lesson I've learned in life is to just be yourself. Treasure the magnificent being that you are and recognize first and foremost you're not here as a human being only. You're a spiritual being having a human experience."
 – **Wayne Dyer**

56. "I just want to do God's will. And He's allowed me to go to the mountain. And I've looked over, and I've seen the promised land! I may not get there with you, but I want you to know tonight that we as a people will get to the promised land."
 – **Martin Luther King, Jr.**

57. "Keep your thoughts positive because your thoughts become your words. Keep your words positive because your words become your behaviors. Keep your behaviors positive because your behaviors become your habits. Keep your habits positive because your habits become your values. Keep your values positive because your values become your destiny."
 – **Mahatma Ghandi**

58. "When you judge another, you do not define them, you define yourself." – **Wayne Dyer**

59. "If you realized how powerful your thoughts are, you would never think a negative thought." – **Peace Pilgrim**

60. "The spirit is one of the most neglected parts of man by doctors and scientists around the world. Yet, it is as vital to our health as the heart and mind. It's time for science to examine the many facets of the soul. The condition of our soul is usually the source of many sicknesses."

    – **Suzy Kassem**

61. "Meditation is the ultimate mobile device; you can use it anywhere, anytime, unobtrusively." – **Sharon Salzberg**

62. "It is in the balancing of your spirituality with your humanity that you will find immeasurable happiness, success, good health, and love." – **Steve Maraboli**

63. "Man is more miserable, more restless and unsatisfied than ever before, simply because half his nature--the spiritual--is starving for true food, and the other half--the material--is fed with bad food." – **Paul Brunton**

64. "The spiritual journey is individual, highly personal. It can't be organized or regulated. It isn't true that everyone should follow one path. Listen to your own truth." – **Ram Dass**

65. "A man can no more diminish God's glory by refusing to worship Him than a lunatic can put out the sun by scribbling the word 'darkness' on the walls of his cell." – **C.S. Lewis**

66. "God is whispering in your heart, in the whole existence, just tune your ears." – **Amit Ray**

67. "The Christian does not think God will love us because we are good, but that God will make us good because He loves us." – **C.S. Lewis**

68. "Science without religion is lame, religion without science is blind." – **Albert Einstein**

69. "That... man... says women can't have as much rights as man, cause Christ wasn't a woman. Where did your Christ come from? . . . From God and a woman. Man had nothing to do with him." – **Sojourner Truth**

70. "My hope for my children must be that they respond to the still, small voice of God in their own hearts."
    – **Andrew Young**

71. "Anyone who thinks sitting in church can make you a Christian must also think that sitting in a garage can make you a car." – **Garrison Keillor**

72. "I believe in Christianity as I believe that the sun has risen: not only because I see it, but because by it I see everything else." – **C.S. Lewis**

73. "Prayer is not asking. It is a longing of the soul. It is daily admission of one's weakness. It is better in prayer to have a heart without words than words without a heart."
    – **Mahatma Gandhi**

74. "My concern is not whether God is on our side; my greatest concern is to be on God's side, for God is always right."
    – **Abraham Lincoln**

75. "All I have seen teaches me to trust the Creator for all I have not seen." – **Ralph Waldo Emerson**

76. "God allows us to experience the low points of life in order to teach us lessons that we could learn in no other way."
    – C.S. Lewis

77. "No woman wants to be in submission to a man who isn't in submission to God!" – **T.D. Jakes**

78. "A baby is God's opinion that the world should go on."
    – **Carl Sandburg**

79. "We have one life; it soon will be past; what we do for God is all that will last." – **Muhammad Ali**

80. "It takes three to make love, not two: you, your spouse, and God. Without God people only succeed in bringing out the worst in one another. Lovers who have nothing else to do but love each other soon find there is nothing else. Without a central loyalty life is unfinished." – **Fulton J. Sheen**

81. "I'm not afraid of death because I don't believe in it. It's just getting out of one car, and into another." – **John Lennon**

82. "Through hard work, perseverance and a faith in God, you can live your dreams." – **Ben Carson**

83. "I am convinced that the jealous, the angry, the bitter and the egotistical are the first to race to the top of mountains. A confident person enjoys the journey, the people they meet along the way and sees life not as a competition. They reach the summit last because they know God isn't at the top waiting for them. He is down below helping his followers to understand that the view is glorious where ever you stand."
 – **Shannon L. Alder**

84. "More smiling, less worrying. More compassion, less judgment. More blessed, less stressed. More love, less hate."
 – **Roy T. Bennett**

85. "I distrust those people who know so well what God wants them to do because I notice it always coincides with their own desires." – **Susan B. Anthony**

86. "We are not human beings having a spiritual experience. We are spiritual beings having a human experience."
 – **Pierre Teilhard de Chardin**

87. "The first peace, which is the most important, is that which comes within the souls of people when they realize their relationship, their oneness with the universe and all its powers, and when they realize at the center of the universe dwells the Great Spirit, and that its center is really everywhere, it is within each of us." – **Black Elk**

88. "It does not matter how long you are spending on the earth, how much money you have gathered or how much attention you have received. It is the amount of positive vibration you have radiated in life that matters," – **Amit Ray**

89. "Each star is a mirror reflecting the truth inside you." – **Aberjhani**

90. "A sacrifice to be real must cost, must hurt, and must empty ourselves. Give yourself fully to God. He will use you to accomplish great things on the condition that you believe much more in his love than in your weakness."
    – **Mother Teresa**

91. "Your sacred space is where you can find yourself over and over again." – **Joseph Campbell**

92. "Believe in your infinite potential. Your only limitations are those you set upon yourself." – **Roy T. Bennett**

93. "Once upon a time, I dreamt I was a butterfly, fluttering hither and thither, to all intents and purposes a butterfly. I was conscious only of my happiness as a butterfly, unaware that I was myself. Soon I awaked, and there I was, veritably myself again. Now I do not know whether I was then a man dreaming I was a butterfly, or whether I am now a butterfly, dreaming I am a man." – **Zhuangzi**

94. "The reality of loving God is loving him like he's a Superhero who actually saved you from stuff rather than a Santa Claus who merely gave you some stuff." – **Criss Jami**

95. "If a man is to live, he must be all alive, body, soul, mind, heart, spirit." – **Thomas Merton**

96. "These things will destroy the human race: politics without principle, progress without compassion, wealth without work, learning without silence, religion without fearlessness, and worship without awareness." – **Anthony de Mello**

97. "Love goes very far beyond the physical person of the beloved. It finds its deepest meaning in his spiritual being, his inner self. Whether or not he is actually present, whether or not he is still alive at all, ceases somehow to be of importance." – **Viktor E. Frankl**

98. "The soul is like an uninhabited world that comes to life only when God lays His head against us." – **Thomas Aquinas**

99. "God loved us before he made us; and his love has never diminished and never shall." – **Julian of Norwich**

100. "Pray as though everything depended on God. Work as though everything depended on you." – **Saint Augustine**

SUMMARY: Spirituality

Invest in your spiritual development. First Thessalonians 5:23 reminds us that we are made up of spirit, soul, and body, and we need to attend to all three. We must not be overly consumed with things in the natural realm. Romans 8:6 says, "For to be carnally minded is death, but to be spiritually minded is life and peace."

I recommend reading the Bible and spending lots of time in prayer to help your spirit mature.

The forest not only hides man's enemies but it's full of man's medicine, healing power and food.

~African Proverb

SIX

HEALTH

There's no better time like the present to make a change by committing to a healthier lifestyle. Healthy eating, healing with foods, and not indulging in drugs and alcohol are essential to keeping your body and mind strong and functioning properly. The body heals itself when you treat it right; but sometimes it takes longer to heal because you continue to abuse it by indulging in the wrong things over and over. So, as your body heals you've got to modify your lifestyle. Improve your eating habits and your sleeping habits and this will transform your body and mind by giving it the nutrients that it needs.

In ancient times - biblical times - God came to people in their dreams. The ancient people and the American Indians really believed in their dreams; but today, we don't really pay much attention to them and to the things that happen in our subconscious world. Ideas that reflect around our health often come into our dreams and try to correct our personality and change our bad habits. But, if we don't adhere to the ideas and make those changes, we go to the doctor trying to have him or her intervene for us because we haven't paid any attention to our subconscious.

National Baseball Hall of Fame inductee and former left fielder for St. Louis Cardinals, **Lou Brock** stated: "To be successful in life, you must have a dream. Stay within your bounds and let your passion take over. Your health can affect your ability to fulfill your dreams. To stay

Health

healthy, one of the things I would be concerned with is high blood sugar count or low blood sugar count. I played baseball for about 18 years with diabetes. I was about 23 when I was diagnosed. It's something that sneaks up on you. I actually went blind for about a week and I went to the doctor and discovered that I had a high blood sugar count of about 800. The doctor said to me, "If you don't get your blood count down you are gone." That's the reality with a lot of people. There aren't any symptoms, until it's full blown. Sometimes people feel bad and think maybe tomorrow I'll feel better. But it sneaks up on you, so don't ignore it when you feel bad – it can happen at any age. Form good eating habits, stay healthy and always think about fair play, sports have a way of governing you; so, if it's your passion, let it define you. When that happens, know the limit of where you can go."

Unfortunately, if you do ignore the signals too long you will have to visit a doctor, but the doctor does not usually bother to find out the root of the problem, or what happened when this problem started. Doctors seldom ask themselves questions, such as: W*hat's the root of this? What's happening? Why is this happening?* The doctor is probably not going to try to find out, and depending on the problem, will give you a "Band-aid" or topical solution - chemotherapy, a chemical solution or pills – to try to get rid of the problem.

The truth is, you may get rid of the symptoms and the problem for a little while, but if you don't get to the root, it's very likely going to re-occur. Unlike many of the doctors, I am interested in helping people to find out how to keep the body, mind and spirit healthy by paying attention to your subconscious.

First, you should take care of your body by eating right and exercising every day, as much as you can. There are so many foods out there that are no good for us. Food companies take most of the nutrients out of food – everything is pasteurized, homogenized, processed and whatever other names they give to it. Read the labels, you'll know

Your Daily Dose of Quotes and Anecdotes

exactly what I am talking about. Just pay attention - eat healthy, exercise, live healthy and try to do the right things for your body.

Because I work a lot with teens through the Make the Grade Foundation, I am very concerned with specific issues and spend much time challenging them to pay attention to their health. For instance, a good way to keep your weight under control is to participate in physical activities. Health experts recommend that all teens should be active every day as part of play, sports, work, transportation, gym class, or planned exercise. Three or more times each week, teens should do something that requires moderate to high levels of exertion for 20 minutes or more. This may include jogging, brisk walking, swimming, skating, aerobic dance, tennis, and full-court basketball. If you do any of these things, there will be a major difference in how you look and feel.

Stay informed. Talk to knowledgeable people in general. You don't have to be in school, but, to exercise your mind; you can talk to people in authority, people with something intelligent to say. You need to educate yourself every day, in every way possible.

A teen's concern about his or her athletic ability may sometimes lead to both mental and physical problems. For example, teens that are involved in activities that require weight management (such as ballet, wrestling, and gymnastics) may be at a greater risk for the eating disorders anorexia nervosa (self-starvation) or bulimia (binge and purge). Some teens use steroids to build muscle or improve their athletic ability. These are potentially life-threatening behaviors and should be avoided. Instead of focusing on how to "fit-in", focus on how to be healthy and everything else will fall into place.

Former world champion boxer and Olympic Gold Medal Winner **Mark Breland** states, *Live your dream, follow your path. To reach your full potential in life, it takes hard work and dedication. My mission is to interact with as many children as possible about the*

benefits of healthy eating and staying in shape, both mentally and physically. No partying, no hanging out, no drinking, no drugs and no smoking. A healthy mind and healthy body will give you the tools you need toward achieving a brighter future.

Here are some quick facts that could affect your teen's well-being. Discussing these facts and their associated perils could save your teen's life:

- Injuries kill more teens than all diseases combined.
- Car crashes are one of the leading causes of death and disability among teens today.
- At least one teen dies of an injury every hour every day in the United States.
- Other causes of injury or death among teens include drowning, sports injuries, and rape.
- More teens are being killed by guns than ever before.
- Most teens do not like and do not wear bike helmets.
- Adolescents are less likely to use seat belts than any other age group.
- Understanding and obeying the rules of the road are important components of safe cycling.
- Alcohol is involved in about 35% of teen driver fatalities
- Healthy eating means healthy living.
- School nurses are beginning to see more students with health problems associated with the piercing of various body parts.
- Health experts recommend that all teens should be active every day as part of play, sports, work, transportation, gym class, or planned exercise.
- Healthy eating, healing with foods, and doing the proper things are essential because the body heals itself when you treat it right.
- A death in the family, illness, divorce or change in environment can negatively affect a child's behavior.

BOB'S 100 FAVORITE QUOTES ABOUT HEALTH

1. "To keep the body in good health is a duty... otherwise we shall not be able to keep our mind strong and clear." – **Buddha**

2. "It is health that is real wealth and not pieces of gold and silver." – **Mahatma Gandhi**

3. "Early to bed and early to rise makes a man healthy, wealthy and wise." – **Benjamin Franklin**

4. "Sleep is that golden chain that ties health and our bodies together." – **Thomas Dekker**

5. "I believe that the greatest gift you can give your family and the world is a healthy you." – **Joyce Meyer**

6. "Good health is not something we can buy. However, it can be an extremely valuable savings account."
    – **Anne Wilson Schaef**

7. "When wealth is lost, nothing is lost; when health is lost, something is lost; when character is lost, all is lost."
    – **Billy Graham**

8. "You know, all that really matters is that the people you love are happy and healthy. Everything else is just sprinkles on the sundae." – **Paul Walker**

9. "There's nothing more important than our good health - that's our principal capital asset." – **Arlen Specter**

10. "Treasure the love you receive above all. It will survive long after your good health has vanished." – **Og Mandino**

11. "My personal goals are to be happy, healthy and to be surrounded by loved ones." – **Kiana Tom**

12. "He who has health, has hope; and he who has hope, has everything." – **Thomas Carlyle**

13. "It's better to be healthy alone than sick with someone else."
    – **Phil McGraw**

14. "When you are young and healthy, it never occurs to you that in a single second your whole life could change."
    – **Annette Funicello**
15. "Looking after my health today gives me a better hope for tomorrow." – **Anne Wilson Schaef**
16. "You know, true love really matters, friends really matter, family really matters. Being responsible and disciplined and healthy really matters." – **Courtney Thorne-Smith**
17. "As I see it, every day you do one of two things: build health or produce disease in yourself." – **Adelle Davis**
18. "A lot of times growing up you don't want to eat your green beans, and your spinach, and all the other healthy things that you should eat. So, I would encourage young people to do that. And get outside! What is hurting young people today is that video games are killing us because we don't get outside like we used to." – **Earvin Magic Johnson**
19. "If you neglect to recharge a battery, it dies. And if you run full speed ahead without stopping for water, you lose momentum to finish the race." – **Oprah Winfrey**
20. "I made a commitment to completely cut out drinking and anything that might hamper me from getting my mind and body together. And the floodgates of goodness have opened upon me - spiritually and financially." – **Denzel Washington**
21. "First of all, I'm happy that I'm healthy." – **Tina Turner**
22. "As long as there is poverty in the world I can never be rich, even if I have a billion dollars. As long as diseases are rampant and millions of people in this world cannot expect to live more than twenty-eight or thirty years, I can never be totally healthy even if I just got a good checkup at Mayo Clinic. I can never be what I ought to be until you are what you ought to be. This is the way our world is made. No individual or nation can stand out boasting of being independent. We are interdependent."
    – **Martin Luther King, Jr**.

23. "Water is colourless and tasteless but you can live on it longer than eating food." – **African Proverb**

24. "The best of mankind is a farmer; the best food is fruit." – **Ethiopian Proverb**

25. "Dieting is the only game where you win when you lose." – **Karl Lagerfield**

26. "Your imagination is your preview to life's coming attractions." – **Albert Einstein**

27. "A fit, healthy body-- that is the best fashion statement." – **Jess C. Scott**

28. "The higher your energy level, the more efficient your body. The more efficient your body, the better you feel and the more you will use your talent to produce outstanding results."
– **Anthony Robbins**

29. "Take care of your body. It's the only place you have to live."
– **Jim Rohn**

30. "The groundwork of all happiness is health." – **Leigh Hunt**

31. "Health is a state of complete physical, mental and social well-being, and not merely the absence of disease or infirmity."
– **World Health Organization**

32. "The longer I live the less confidence I have in drugs and the greater is my confidence in the regulation and administration of diet and regimen." – **John Redman Coxe**

33. "A good laugh and a long sleep are the best cures in the doctor's book." – **Irish Proverb**

34. "Health is a large word. It embraces not the body only, but the mind and spirit as well; and not today's pain or pleasure alone, but the whole being and outlook of a man.
– **James H. West**

59. "Eating crappy food isn't a reward -- it's a punishment." – **Drew Carey**

60. "It is important to keep in mind that our bodies must work pretty well, or there wouldn't be so many humans on the planet." – **Ina May Gaskin**

61. "The body is wiser than its inhabitants. the body is the soul. the body is god's messenger." – **Erica Jong**

62. "The best diet is the one you don't know you're on." – **Brian Wansink**

63. "Health nuts are going to feel stupid someday, lying in hospitals dying of nothing..." – **Redd Foxx**

64. Live Life Fully & Abundantly. – **Gabbriella Conte**

65. If you can show people how to build castles, make sure you do not neglect building and nurturing your own.
    – **Suzy Kassem**

66. "When our emotional health is in a bad state, so is our level of self-esteem. We have to slow down and deal with what is troubling us, so that we can enjoy the simple joy of being happy and at peace with ourselves." – **Jess C. Scott**

67. "The most poetical thing in the world is not being sick." – **G.K. Chesterton**

68. "About eighty percent of the food on shelves of supermarkets today didn't exist 100 years ago." – **Larry McCleary**

69. "Your emotional state has a tremendous amount to do with sickness, health and well-being. For years, my husband and I lived on -- and because of -- hope. Hope continues to give me the mental strength to carry on." – **Dana Reeve**

70. "Talking about unpleasant things during a meal is not good for digestion, not good for health." – **Betty Jamie Chung**

71. "Be thankful for a breath of fresh air to be alive and well. Allow love and happiness to penetrate throughout your mind and soul. Take time to relax and live in the moment, the now, the present. Enjoy today." – **Amaka Imani Nkosazana**

72. "Tell me what you eat and I will tell you who you are." – **Jean Anthelme Brillat-Savarin**

73. "If there had been an exercise I'd liked, would I have gotten this big in the first place?" – **Jennifer Weiner**

74. "There's no dignity, no decency, or health today for men that haven't got a job. All other things depend on work today." – **Nevil Shute**

75. "Words are like food. They contain information that either releases and liberates and creates possibilities and development or locks you into unhealthy patterns you can't change." – **Thorbjörg Hafsteinsdottir**

76. "I knew I wasn't the picture of health, but I didn't think I was headed for the last roundup." – **Fannie Flagg**

77. "Until you believe you can do it, it's going to be difficult to convince anyone else you can do it." – **Toni Sorenson**

78. "None of us know how to fix ourselves, at least not entirely, not well enough." – **Catherine Lacey**

79. "If you keep on eating unhealthy food than no matter how many weight loss tips you follow, you are likely to retain weight and become obese. If only you start eating healthy food, you will be pleasantly surprised how easy it is to lose weight." – **Subodh Gupta**

80. "There is no illness that is not exacerbated by stress." – **Allan Lokos**

81. "You only get one body; it is the temple of your soul. Even God is willing to dwell there. If you truly treat your body like a temple, it will serve you well for decades. If you abuse it you must be prepared for poor health and a lack of energy." – **Oli Hille**

82. "Eating healthy nutritious food is the simple and right solution to get rid of excess body weight effortlessly and become slim and healthy forever." – **Subodh Gupta**

83. "Never take today for granted, tomorrow might never come." – **Matt Vella**

84. "Humor and Health, The staples of wealth." – **S Austin**

85. "I believe that love and forgiveness engages an incomprehensible healing force and sometimes true healing occurs, but always an emotional and spiritual healing happens." – **Angeli Maun Akey**

86. "Health is the natural condition. When sickness occurs, it is a sign that Nature has gone off course because of a physical or mental imbalance. The road to health for everyone is through moderation, harmony, and a 'sound mind in a sound body'." – **Jostein Gaarder**

87. "The healthy man is the thin man. But you don't need to go hungry for it: Remove the flours, starches and sugars; that's all." – **Samael Aun Weor**

88. "Health and disease are the same thing—vital action intended to preserve, maintain, and protect the body. There is no more reason for treating disease than there is for treating health." – **Herbert M. Shelton**

89. "Health is more than the absence of disease. Health is about jobs and employment, education, the environment, and all of those things that go into making us healthy." – **Joycelyn Elders**

90. "Walk 1 and Drink 8. Walk 1 km and drink 8 cups of water every day. Pass it on!" – **Clive Scarff**

91. "Moderation is the only rule of a healthful life. This means moderation in all things wholesome." – **Herbert M. Shelton**

92. "Gym is a sacred place which makes your life feel worth existing by putting effort of care into the home of your soul called body!" – **Munia Khan**

93. "If you have health, you probably will be happy, and if you have health and happiness, you have all the wealth you need, even if it is not all you want." – **Elbert Hubbard**

94. "That is what chronic illness is . . . a disconnect between what our souls can do and what our bodies can do." – **Barbara Lieberman**

95. "Getting healthy will always result in weight loss as a side effect, but a side effect of dieting and weight loss is often poorer health." – **Christopher Earle**

96. A well-lived day is medicine unto itself. – **Acharya Shunya**

97. "Eating organic for good health and spending your day sitting down using a wireless computer that is next to a WiFi router is a classic case of Yin & Yang." – **Steven Magee**

98. "Always walk as if you're running late, it's healthier." – **Benny Bellamacina**

99. "Health is Wealth." – **Ronnie Plant**

100. "Of course, I want to be number one. But being happy and healthy is the most important thing." – **Venus Williams**

SUMMARY: Health

In order to experience a dynamic life, you must take care of your health. The Christian faith honors that. In Third John 1:2 it says: "Dear friend, I pray that you may enjoy good health and that all may go well with you, even as your soul is getting along well."

We must give attention to our physical condition.

Too many people spend money they haven't earned, to buy things they don't want, to impress people they don't like.
– Will Smith

SEVEN

FINANCIAL LITERACY

I had a great mentor in Percy Sutton. He was an Intelligence Officer with the Tuskegee Airmen, an attorney, a politician, cofounder of Inner City Broadcasting Corporation and my dear friend. One of the things he used to tell me was, *I keep about 5 or 6 or 7 businesses because if 1 or 2 or 3 or even 4 fail I'm still in business.* That's a serious quote, and to this day, I rely on his wisdom to guide me through many of my financial decisions. I have many facets to my life, but I am confident that I always use my time wisely and I constantly look to the future.

When many students graduate from college they are already in debt, because their parents may not have been able to save for their college education. But for those students whose parents are able to save tuition for them, by the time they graduate, they are well on their way. It's also important, when somebody gives you a financial contract to know how many years you are going into it and what you must do to honor the terms.

According to award-winning Financial Advisor, Ryan Mack, "In today's economy it's more important than ever to make sure you borrow wisely by planning for the future and only borrowing what you can afford.

Talk to your children about the principles of financial literacy as early as 6 or 7 years old. By the time they are in 1st or 2nd grade they should begin to have conversations about the allocation of money. When I was a little kid, I used to think there was a midget inside the ATM machine dispensing money and my mother told me "No I have to work to put money into my bank account in order to get money out of the bank." She made me understand that she had to work to put money in and couldn't just pull it out. Having conversations like I had with my mother can teach children how important banking is.

When parents get their children to think about where their money is going, it can lead to a larger conversation about budgeting before spending. Sometimes parents are hesitant to discuss credit with their children because they may be going through personal financial challenges themselves. But it never hurts to be honest and I feel that having open discussions about financial literacy is beneficial to the child, as well as to the parent. From the time they are toddlers, children can learn by playing number games and paying the cashier when purchases are being made at the store.

In the higher grades, when students need it the most, the teachers don't teach the students all those things that are necessary to financially sustain them throughout their lives.

Dr. Boyce Watkins, author, economist, political analyst and social commentator shared some important facts about financial planning: "From everything I've heard and read both publicly and privately, the singer Prince (aka Prince Rogers Nelson) was three things: Conscientious, humble and extremely intelligent…but even the wisest among us can make mistakes. One mistake Prince made was that he didn't leave a will before he died. This has led to complete chaos as every long-lost relative, distant friend and associate has been jockeying for a chance to get a piece of his estate. Prince's error is one that is made by millions of African Americans, so there is no shame in his mistake. But the fact is that we MUST correct this issue right now.

One of the secrets of Black Financial Intelligence taught to me by my grandmother is to make sure that you do all you can to prepare for your own passing. Many African American families, because we have a fear of discussing death, often live as if we're never going to die. Then, when death ALWAYS comes, our loved ones are left suffering due to a lack of planning by those who didn't care enough to make plans for the afterlife.

It's never too early to start preparing for your future; but for many of us, too often it's too late. Throughout the various stages of your life, there should be a thought process and an evaluation about what you have, what you want and what you need. Money is the common thread but it's not the end all. How you get it, how you maintain it, how you keep it and how you increase it is not about guessing, it's about planning. To journey through life the best way possible, I advise you to ask questions, read books, attend seminars, talk to a financial advisor, hire an accountant, know your limitations and follow the rules.

If you stick with something long enough, something always happens…but make sure it's positive. Follow your dreams. Find out what you want to do in life and you will Make the Grade.

BOB'S 100 FAVORITE QUOTES ABOUT FINANCIAL LITERACY

1. "Money and success don't change people; they merely amplify what is already there." – **Will Smith**

2. "Money doesn't buy happiness. Some people say it's a heck of a down payment, though." – **Denzel Washington**

3. "When you control a man's thinking you do not have to worry about his actions." – **Dr. Carter G. Woodson**

4. "Make sure you get involved in something that you really enjoy doing because you're going to have to work for the rest of your life." – **Bob Lee**

5. "If the Negro in the ghetto must eternally be fed by the hand that pushes him into the ghetto, he will never become strong enough to get out of the ghetto." – **Dr. Carter G. Woodson**

6. "If there is no struggle, there is no progress. Those who profess to favor freedom, and yet depreciate agitation, are men who want crops without plowing up the ground. They want rain without thunder and lightning. They want the ocean without the awful roar of its many waters. This struggle may be a moral one; or it may be a physical one; or it may be both moral and physical; but it must be a struggle."

    – **Frederick Douglass**

7. "At the bottom of education, at the bottom of politics, even at the bottom of religion, there must be for our race economic independence." – **Booker T. Washington**

8. "There is no force like success, and that is why the individual makes all effort to surround himself throughout life with the evidence of it; as of the individual, so should it be of the nation." – **Marcus Garvey**

9. "So, our people not only have to be reeducated to the importance of supporting black business, but the black man himself has to be made aware of the importance of going into business. And once you and I go into business, we own and

operate at least the businesses in our community. What we will be doing is developing a situation wherein we will actually be able to create employment for the people in the community. And once you can create some employment in the community where you live it will eliminate the necessity of you and me having to act ignorantly and disgracefully, boycotting and picketing some practice someplace else trying to beg him for a job." – **Malcolm X**

10. "Business opportunities are like buses, there's always another one coming." – **Richard Branson**

11. "When you want to win, you have to do the right thing…prepare before you get there." – **Bob Lee**

12. "I don't stand for black man's side, I don't stand for white man's side, I stand for God's side." – **Bob Marley**

13. "I don't think it is an exaggeration to say that financial literacy, economic empowerment, and wealth building is going to be the last leg of the civil rights movement. Because one step toward financial literacy takes you two steps toward personal empowerment**." – Russell Simmons**

14. "It is a call for black people in this country to unite, to recognize their heritage, to build a sense of community. It is a call for black people to define their own goals, to lead their own organizations." – **Stokely Carmichael**

15. "People seem to be coming around to the idea that true freedom as an economic foundation and that economic development is in fact connected to the development of Black privately-owned business." – **George Subira**

16. "One thing that's true is that whether you are making a financial investment or an investment of the heart, you usually get what you give. What's also true is that investing the wrong assets into the wrong places is a great way to end up broke (or broken)." – **Dr. Boyce Watkins**

17. "When you get knocked down, just get up and keep moving forward…there are a lot of hurdles in life…but there are a lot of heroes who get over those hurdles." – **Bob Lee**

18. "Any time you stop producing and focus only on consuming, you have nothing to be proud of, other than what you consume…if you don't produce and wait on someone to hire you, and give you a vision, you may not get there… and until we start taking over our community understanding our marketplace and get our lion's share of the marketplace, we will never get up." – **Bishop T.D. Jakes**

19. "Over a seven-year period, I can tell you unequivocally wealth is not a function of gender, not a function of race. It is not a function of circumstance. It is not a function of condition—how the cards were dealt, which side of the town you were born on, but it is a function of choice, a function of discipline, and it is a function of effort, faith, and believing in yourself." – **Dr. Dennis Kimbro**

20. "Do not be embarrassed by your failures, learn from them and start again." – **Richard Branson**

21. "If you stick with something long enough, something always happens…but make sure it's positive. Follow your dreams. Find out what you want to do in life and you, too, will Make the Grade." – **Bob Lee**

22. "A man can be as great as he wants to be. If you believe in yourself and have the courage, the determination, the dedication, the competitive drive and if you are willing to sacrifice the little things in life and pay the price for the things that are worthwhile, it can be done."
    – **Vince Lombardi**

23. "Do not call for black power or green power. Call for brain power." **Barbara Jordan**

24. "Surround yourself with people who take their work seriously, but not themselves, those who work hard and play hard." – **Colin Powell**

25. "Success is to be measured not so much by the position that one has reached in life as by the obstacles which he has overcome while trying to succeed." – **Booker T. Washington**

26. "Normal is getting dressed in clothes that you buy for work, driving through traffic in a car that you are still paying for, in order to get to a job that you need so you can pay for the clothes, car and the house that you leave empty all day in order to afford to live in it." – **Ellen Goodman**

27. "Money is like the waters of a sailing river it flows away." – **African Proverb**

28. "Everybody wants to be famous, but nobody wants to do the work. I live by that. You grind hard so you can play hard. At the end of the day, you put all the work in, and eventually it'll pay off. It could be in a year, it could be in 30 years. Eventually, your hard work will pay off." – **Kevin Hart**

29. "Better to aim at comfort' than at luxury." – **African Proverb**

30. "It can be liberating to get fired because you realize the world doesn't end. There's other ways to make money, better jobs." – **Ron Livingston**

31. "Even if you're rich, you cannot bury yourself."
    – **African Proverb**

32. "In this world, nothing can be said to be certain, except death and taxes." – **Benjamin Franklin**

33. "Beware of little expenses. A small leak will sink a great ship." – **Benjamin Franklin**

34. "What is sweet in a fool's mouth will surely finish his money."
    – **African Proverb**

35. "Our incomes are like our shoes; if too small, they gall and pinch us; but if too large, they cause us to stumble and to trip." – **John Locke**

36. "Your brother's pocket cannot keep your wealth."
    – **African Proverb**

37. "Wealth consists not in having great possessions, but in having few wants." – **Epictetus**

38. "At this moment, then, the Negroes must begin to do the very thing which they have been taught that they cannot do." – **Carter G. Woodson**

39. "Put your heart, mind, and soul into even your smallest acts. This is the secret of success." – **Swami Sivananda**

40. "A strong, positive self-image is the best possible preparation for success." – **Joyce Brothers**

41. "Try not to become a man of success, but rather try to become a man of value." – **Albert Einstein**

42. "The price of success is hard work, dedication to the job at hand, and the determination that whether we win or lose, we have applied the best of ourselves to the task at hand."
    – **Vince Lombardi**

43. "However difficult life may seem, there is always something you can do and succeed at." – **Stephen Hawking**

44. "Well, I think that there's a very thin dividing line between success and failure. And I think if you start a business without financial backing, you're likely to go the wrong side of that dividing line." – **Richard Branson**

45. "The road to success is not easy to navigate, but with hard work, drive and passion, it's possible to achieve the American dream." – **Tommy Hilfiger**

46. "Money won't create success, the freedom to make it will." – **Nelson Mandela**

47. "Success is not a destination, but the road that you're on. Being successful means that you're working hard and walking your walk every day. You can only live your dream by working hard towards it. That's living your dream."
– **Marlon Wayans**

48. "Without continual growth and progress, such words as improvement, achievement, and success have no meaning."
– **Benjamin Franklin**

49. "You don't want to have so much money going toward your mortgage every month that you can't enjoy life or take care of your other financial responsibilities." – **Dave Ramsey**

50. "It's cheaper to buy a house and finance it than it is to rent in many markets." – **Barry Sternlicht**

51. "Money you won't need to use for at least seven years is money for investing. The goal here is to have your account grow over time to help you finance a distant goal, such as building a retirement fund. Since your goal is in the future, money for investing belongs in stocks." – **Suze Orman**

52. "I like eating out. I like buying beautiful paintings and being surrounded by beautiful things. I have to finance that life. I can barely afford a pension scheme because I don't make enough money." – **Andrew Motion**

53. "A budget tells us what we can't afford, but it doesn't keep us from buying it." – **William Feather**

54. "Financial literacy is an issue that should command our attention because many Americans are not adequately organizing finances for their education, healthcare and retirement." – **Ron Lewis**

55. "The only way you will ever permanently take control of your financial life is to dig deep and fix the root problem."
– **Suze Orman**

56. "Starting out to make money is the greatest mistake in life. Do what you feel you have a flair for doing, and if you are good enough at it, the money will come." **– Greer Garson**

57. "We learned about honesty and integrity - that the truth matters... that you don't take shortcuts or play by your own set of rules... and success doesn't count unless you earn it fair and square." **– Michelle Obama**

58. "At the end of the day, the most overwhelming key to a child's success is the positive involvement of parents." **– Jane D. Hull**

59. "Focused, hard work is the real key to success. Keep your eyes on the goal, and just keep taking the next step towards completing it. If you aren't sure which way to do something, do it both ways and see which works better."
 – John Carmack

60. "There is never just one thing that leads to success for anyone. I feel it always a combination of passion, dedication, hard work, and being in the right place at the right time."
 – Lauren Conrad

61. "Humility is the true key to success. Successful people lose their way at times. They often embrace and overindulge from the fruits of success. Humility halts this arrogance and self-indulging trap. Humble people share the credit and wealth, remaining focused and hungry to continue the journey of success." **– Rick Pitino**

62. "One important key to success is self-confidence. An important key to self-confidence is preparation."
 – Arthur Ashe

63. "I'm always asked, 'What's the secret to success?' But there are no secrets. Be humble. Be hungry. And always be the hardest worker in the room." **– Dwayne Johnson**

64. "All life demands struggle. Those who have everything given to them become lazy, selfish, and insensitive to the real values

of life. The very striving and hard work that we so constantly try to avoid is the major building block in the person we are today." – **Pope Paul VI**

65. "Believe in yourself, and the rest will fall into place. Have faith in your own abilities, work hard, and there is nothing you cannot accomplish." – **Brad Henry**

66. "It's all about quality of life and finding a happy balance between work and friends and family." – **Philip Green**

67. "Pleasure in the job puts perfection in the work." – **Aristotle**

68. "If you're trying to achieve, there will be roadblocks. I've had them; everybody has had them. But obstacles don't have to stop you. If you run into a wall, don't turn around and give up. Figure out how to climb it, go through it, or work around it." – **Michael Jordan**

69. "Work like you don't need the money. Love like you've never been hurt. Dance like nobody's watching." – **Satchel Paige**

70. "Choose a job you love, and you will never have to work a day in your life." – **Confucius**

71. "Stay true to yourself, yet always be open to learn. Work hard, and never give up on your dreams, even when nobody else believes they can come true but you. These are not clichés but real tools you need no matter what you do in life to stay focused on your path." – **Phillip Sweet**

72. "Formal education will make you a living; self-education will make you a fortune." – **Jim Rohn**

73. "Work hard for what you want because it won't come to you without a fight. You have to be strong and courageous and know that you can do anything you put your mind to. If somebody puts you down or criticizes you, just keep on believing in yourself and turn it into something positive." – **Leah LaBelle**

74. "Your work is going to fill a large part of your life, and the only way to be truly satisfied is to do what you believe is great

work. And the only way to do great work is to love what you do. If you haven't found it yet, keep looking. Don't settle. As with all matters of the heart, you'll know when you find it."
– Steve Jobs

75. "Keep your dreams alive. Understand to achieve anything requires faith and belief in yourself, vision, hard work, determination, and dedication. Remember all things are possible for those who believe." **– Gail Devers**

76. "The successful man will profit from his mistakes and try again in a different way." **– Dale Carnegie**

77. "Whatever obstacle comes your way, you gotta be prepared to jump over it! And I think that's what separates the legends from the regular artists. It's all in how you manage that success, and how you deal with the controversy when it actually comes."
– Akon

78. "I do not know anyone who has got to the top without hard work. That is the recipe. It will not always get you to the top, but should get you pretty near." **– Margaret Thatcher**

79. "My mother inspired me to treat others as I would want to be treated regardless of age, race or financial status."
– Tommy Hilfiger

80. "If you don't have the money management skills yet, using a debit card will ensure you don't overspend and rack up debt on a credit card." **– T. Harv Eker**

81. "Money coming in says I've made the right marketing decisions." **– Adam Osborne**

82. "I think the person who takes a job in order to live - that is to say, for the money - has turned himself into a slave."
– Joseph Campbell

83. "So, my happiness doesn't come from money or fame. My happiness comes from seeing life without struggle."
– Nicki Minaj

84. "Let us more and more insist on raising funds of love, of kindness, of understanding, of peace. Money will come if we seek first the Kingdom of God - the rest will be given."
   – Mother Teresa

85. "There is only one boss. The customer. And he can fire everybody in the company from the chairman on down, simply by spending his money somewhere else."
   – Sam Walton

86. "Money has never made man happy, nor will it, there is nothing in its nature to produce happiness. The more of it one has the more one wants." **– Benjamin Franklin**

87. "Sometimes your best investments are the ones you don't make." **– Donald Trump**

88. "A successful man is one who makes more money than his wife can spend. A successful woman is one who can find such a man." **– Lana Turner**

89. "Never confuse the size of your paycheck with the size of your talent." **– Marlon Brando**

90. "The first time you marry for love, the second for money, and the third for companionship." **– Jackie Kennedy**

91. "Money without brains is always dangerous."
   – Napoleon Hill

92. "God wants us to prosper financially, to have plenty of money, to fulfill the destiny He has laid out for us."
   – Joel Osteen

93. "Success isn't measured by money or power or social rank. Success is measured by your discipline and inner peace." – **Mike Ditka**

94. "Surround yourself with the dreamers and the doers, the believers and thinkers, but most of all, surround yourself with those who see the greatness within you, even when you don't see it yourself." **– Edmund Lee**

95. "Nothing stops the man who desires to achieve. Every obstacle is simply a course to develop his achievement muscle. It's a strengthening of his powers of accomplishment."
– **Thomas Carlyle**

96. The greatest thing I ever was able to do was give back a welfare check that I got and said here I don't need this anymore. – **Whoopi Goldberg**

97. "The man who won't loan money isn't going to have many friends - or need them." – **Wilt Chamberlain**

98. "God gives nothing to those who keep their arms crossed." – **African proverb**

99. "Do not pray for tasks equal to your powers, pray for Powers equal to your tasks." – **Phillips Brooks**

100. "Wake up and Smell the Dollars! Whose Inner City is This Anyway!" – **Dorothy Pitman Hughes**

SUMMARY: Financial Literacy

It is critically important that you become a good steward of money. Financial literacy is the place to begin.

Avoid all shortcuts and "get rich quick" tactics. Proverbs 13:11 says, "Dishonest money dwindles away, but whoever gathers money little by little makes it grow." Make sure you learn to save, even little by little, and make financial literacy a topic of study.

PART TWO

MEMORABLE QUOTES
WITH MEANINGFUL MESSAGES

Preparation, Inspiration, Change, Forgiveness,
Acceptance, Success, Challenges, Confidence, Integrity,
Love & Friendship

Your Daily Dose of Quotes and Anecdotes

PREPARATION

Life, for me, wasn't always easy. But, because my father was such a great role model, he taught us to remain positive and to be prepared for whatever life would bring. I wasn't a dreamer; I was a driver who led the way, wanting to be a positive example to my siblings. My message to them was simply: "Prepare before you get there!"

1. "To be prepared for war is one of the most effective means of preserving peace." – **George Washington**

2. "Through perseverance many people win success out of what seemed destined to be certain failure." – **Benjamin Disraeli**

3. "If you define your purpose, learn from your mistakes and find great role models, your journey toward making the grade will be a lot easier." – **Bob Lee**

4. "The best preparation for tomorrow is doing your best today." – **H Jackson Brown Jr.**

5. "If we prepare our preparation should not be too late." – **Winston Churchill**

6. "Prepare for the unknown by studying how others in the past have coped with the unforeseeable and the unpredictable." – **George S. Patton**

7. "Spectacular achievement is always preceded by unspectacular preparation." – **Robert H. Schuller**

8. "I'm not a threatening black person. To them that's probably why I got hired; but I also got hired because I'm good. I have all the tools." – **Branford Marsalis**

9. "It's better to look ahead and prepare, than to look back and regret." – **Jackie Joyner-Kersee**

10. "People often remark that I'm pretty lucky. Luck is only important in so far as getting the chance to sell yourself at the right moment. After that, you've got to have talent and know how to use it." – **Frank Sinatra**

11. "Things may come to those who wait, but only the things left by those who hustle." – **Abraham Lincoln**

12. "Yesterday is history, tomorrow is a mystery, today is a gift of God, which is why we call it the present." – **Bill Keane**

13. "Greatness is not measured by what a man or woman accomplishes, but by the opposition he or she has overcome to reach his goals." – **Dorothy Height**

14. "How wonderful it is that nobody need wait a single moment before starting to improve the world." – **Anne Frank**

15. "Prepare for the unknown by studying how others in the past have coped with the unforeseeable and the unpredictable." – **George S. Patton**

16. "Give me six hours to chop down a tree and I will spend the first four sharpening the axe." — **Abraham Lincoln**

17. "A strong, positive self-image is the best possible preparation for success." – **Joyce Brothers**

18. "A well-adjusted person is one who makes the same mistake twice without getting nervous." – **Alexander Hamilton**

19. "Just as your car runs more smoothly and requires less energy to go faster and farther when the wheels are in perfect alignment, you perform better when your thoughts, feelings, emotions, goals, and values are in balance." – **Brian Tracy**

20. "Don't lower your expectations to meet your performance. Raise your level of performance to meet your expectations." – **Ralph Marston**

Preparation

21. "For all my friends in the media who like quotes, mark this quote down. From this day on I'd like to be known as 'The Big Aristotle' because Aristotle once said, 'Excellence is not a singular act; it's a habit. You are what you repeatedly do.'"
    – **Shaquille O'Neal**

22. "A life spent making mistakes is not only more honorable, but more useful than a life spent doing nothing."
    – **George Bernard Shaw**

23. "Duty, Honor, Country. Those three hallowed words reverently dictate what you ought to be, what you can be, what you will be." – **Douglas MacArthur**

24. "You must take action now that will move you towards your goals. Develop a sense of urgency in your life."
    – **H. Jackson Brown, Jr.**

25. "Greatness is not measured by what a man or woman accomplishes, but by the opposition he or she has overcome to reach his goals." – **Dorothy Height**

INSPIRATION

1. "With great inspiration, every man can reach their highest potential." – **Lailah Gifty Akita**

2. "The person who tries to live alone will not succeed as a human being. His heart withers if it does not answer another heart. His mind shrinks away if he hears only the echoes of his own thoughts and finds no other inspiration."
   – **Pearl S. Buck**

3. "Just don't give up what you're trying to do. Where there is love and inspiration, I don't think you can go wrong."
   – **Ella Fitzgerald**

4. "Without inspiration, the best powers of the Mind remain dormant; there is a fuel in a switch needs to be ignited with Sparks." – **Johann Gottfried Von Herder**

5. "Perfection is not attainable, but if we chase perfection we can catch excellence." – **Vince Lombardi**

6. "Try to be a rainbow in someone's cloud." – **Maya Angelou**

7. "Nothing is impossible; the word itself says 'I'm possible'!" – **Audrey Hepburn**

8. "It is during our darkest moments that we must focus to see the light." – **Aristotle Onassis**

9. "There are two ways of spreading light: to be the candle or the mirror that reflects it." – **Edith Wharton**

10. "A hero is someone who has given his or her life to something bigger than oneself." Are you a hero?"
    – **Joseph Campbell**

11. "Clouds come floating into my life, no longer to carry rain or usher storm, but to add color to my sunset sky."
    – **Rabindranath Tagore**

22. "Knowledge comes, but wisdom lingers. It may not be difficult to store up in the mind a vast quantity of facts within a comparatively short time, but the ability to form judgments requires the severe discipline of hard work and the tempering heat of experience and maturity." – **Calvin Coolidge**

23. "When you get into a tight place and everything goes against you, till it seems as though you could not hang on a minute longer, never give up then, for that is just the place and time that the tide will turn." – **Harriet Beecher Stowe**

24. "Just as your car runs more smoothly and requires less energy to go faster and farther when the wheels are in perfect alignment, you perform better when your thoughts, feelings, emotions, goals, and values are in balance." – **Brian Tracy**

25. "Nothing can stop the man with the right mental attitude from achieving his goal; nothing on earth can help the man with the wrong mental attitude." – **Thomas Jefferson**

26. "Some people wonder all their lives if they've made a difference. The Marines don't have that problem."
    – **Ronald Reagan**

27. "The truth is incontrovertible. Malice may attack it, ignorance may deride it, but in the end, there it is."
    – **Winston Churchill**

28. "The right to be heard does not automatically include the right to be taken seriously." – **Hubert H. Humphrey**

29. "Prosperity is not without many fears and disasters; and adversity is not without comforts and hopes."
    – **Francis Bacon**

11. "In any moment of decision, the best thing you can do is the right thing and expect that this thing is the wrong thing, and the worst thing you can do is nothing."
    – Theodore Roosevelt

12. "If you're offered a seat on a rocket-ship, don't ask what seat…just get on." **– Sheryl Sandberg**

13. "Be bold, be courageous, be your best." **– Gabrielle Giffords**

14. "Be thankful for what you have; you'll end up having more. If you concentrate on what you don't have, you will never, ever have enough." – **Oprah Winfrey**

15. "Don't worry about failures, worry about the choices you miss when you don't even try." **– Jack Canfield**

16. "Do not let what you cannot do interfere with what you can do." **– John M. Wooden**

17. "You have to have confidence in your ability, and then be tough enough to follow through." **– Rosalyn Carter**

18. "To be a champion you have to believe in yourself when nobody else will." **– Sugar Ray Robinson**

19. "Trust gives you the permission to give people direction, get everyone aligned, and give them the energy to go get the job done. Trust enables you to execute with excellence and produce extraordinary results. As you execute with excellence and deliver on your commitments, trust becomes easier to inspire, creating a flywheel of performance."
    – Douglas Conant

20. "Blessed is he who has learned to admire but not envy, to follow but not imitate, to praise but not flatter, and to lead but not manipulate." **– William Arthur Ward**

21. "Things may come to those who wait, but only the things left by those who hustle." **– Abraham Lincoln**

CONFIDENCE

1. "Our children may learn about heroes of the past; our task is to make ourselves architects of the future." – **Jomo Kenyatta**

2. "I don't believe in Failure. It is not failure if you enjoyed the process." – **Oprah Winfrey**

3. "I used to want the words 'she tried' on my Tombstone. Now I want 'she did it'." – **Katherine Dunham**

4. "If you have no confidence in self you are twice defeated in the race of life, with confidence you have won even before you have started." – **Marcus Garvey**

5. "When you were born, you cried and everybody else was happy, the only question that matters is this; when you die, will you be happy when everyone else is crying."
   – **Tony Campolo**

6. "Speak when you are angry and you make the best speech you'll ever regret." – **Laurence J Peter**

7. "Great ambition is the passion of a Great Character. Those endowed with it may perform very good or very bad acts, all depends on the principles which direct them."
   – **Napoleon Bonaparte**

8. "Obedience brings peace in decision-making. if we have firmly made up our minds to follow the Commandments we will not have to read. Decide which path to take when Temptation comes our way." – **James E Faust**

9. "It is easier to do one's duty to others and to oneself if you do your duty to others you are considered reliable if you do your duty to yourself you are considered selfish."
   – **Thomas Edison**

10. "Vitality shows in not only the ability to persist but the ability to start over." – **F. Scott Fitzgerald**

52. "We must try to share blessings and not miseries."
   – Winston Churchill

53. "Challenge is the pathway to engagement and progress in our lives. But not all challenges are created equal. Some challenges make us feel alive, engaged, connected, and fulfilled. Others simply overwhelm us. Knowing the difference as you set bigger and bolder challenges for yourself is critical to your sanity, success, and satisfaction."
   – Brendon Burchard

54. "A man who has nothing for which he is willing to fight, nothing which is more important than his own personal safety, is a miserable creature and has no chance of being free unless made and kept so by the exertions of better men than himself."
   – John Stuart Mill

55. "It takes a great deal of bravery to stand up to our enemies, but just as much to stand up to our friends." **– J. K. Rowling**

43. "There is no dishonor in losing the race. There is only dishonor in not racing because you are afraid to lose."
   – Garth Stein

44. "A good leader can engage in a debate frankly and thoroughly, knowing that at the end he and the other side must be closer, and thus emerges stronger. You don't have that idea when you are arrogant, superficial, and uninformed." **– Nelson Mandela**

45. "This is no time for ease and comfort, it is the time to do and endure." **– Winston Churchill**

46. "The secret of concentration is the secret of self-discovery. You reach inside yourself to discover your personal resources, and what it takes to match them to the challenge." **– Arnold Palmer**

47. "When you challenge other people's ideas of who or how you should be, they may try to diminish and disgrace you. It can happen in small ways in hidden places, or in big ways on a world stage. You can spend a lifetime resenting the tests, angry about the slights and the injustices. Or, you can rise above it."
   – Carly Fiorina

48. "When you do what you love, the seemingly impossible becomes simply challenging, the laborious becomes purposeful resistance, the difficult loses its edge and is trampled by your progress." **– Steve Maraboli**

49. "Nearly all men can stand adversity, but if you want to test a man's character, give him power." **– Abraham Lincoln**

50. "Experience is not what happens to you; it's what you do with what happens to you." **– Aldous Huxley**

51. "To rejoice in another's prosperity, is to give content to your own lot: to mitigate another's grief, is to alleviate or dispel your own." **– Thomas Edwards**

31. "Do not consider painful what is good for you." – **Euripides**

32. "The only man who never makes a mistake is the man who never does anything." – **Theodore Roosevelt**

33. "No reasonable person could expect us to solve all the problems of the world while we are fighting for our lives."
– **Winston Churchill**

34. "Every tomorrow has two handles. We can take hold of it with the handle of anxiety or the handle of faith."
– **Henry Ward Beecher**

35. "If you expect the world to be fair with you because you are fair with them, it is like expecting a lion not to eat you because you don't eat lion..." – **Unknown**

36. "You will never be happy if you continue to search for what happiness consists of. You will never live if you are looking for the meaning of life." – **Albert Camus**

37. "If you want to make peace with your enemy, you have to work with your enemy. Then he becomes your partner."
– **Nelson Mandela**

38. "Pessimism doesn't grow your business or even maintain the status quo. The pessimists on your staff make the job harder for everyone around them. They make difficulties out of opportunities." – **Harvey Mackay**

39. "How old would you be if you didn't know how old you are?"
– **Satchel Paige**

40. "If you do what you've always done, you'll get what you've always gotten." – **Tony Robbins**

41. "Forget what hurt you in the past. But never forget what it taught you." – **Unknown**

42. "All good is hard. All evil is easy. Dying, losing, cheating, and mediocrity is easy. Stay away from easy."
– **Scott Alexander**

23. "Challenge is the pathway to engagement and progress in our lives. But not all challenges are created equal. Some challenges make us feel alive, engaged, connected, and fulfilled. Others simply overwhelm us. Knowing the difference as you set bigger and bolder challenges for yourself is critical to your sanity, success, and satisfaction."
   – Brendon Burchard

24. "For to be free is not merely to cast off one's chains, but to live in a way that respects and enhances the freedom of others." – **Nelson Mandela**

25. "The problem with thick skin is that it leaves you impervious to the sharpest of pins. Everything becomes dull. But without that sense of pain, there cannot be that sense of relief. Ultimately, the thickened skin leaves you numb, incapable of feeling the highs and lows of life. It leaves you rough like a rock and just as inanimate." – **Michael Soll**

26. "You have enemies? Good. That means you've stood up for something, sometime in your life." – **Winston Churchill**

27. "I advise you to say your dream is possible and then overcome all inconveniences, ignore all the hassles and take a running leap through the hoop, even if it is in flames."
   – Les Brown

28. "I can control my destiny, but not my fate. Destiny means there are opportunities to turn right or left, but fate is a one-way street. I believe we all have the choice as to whether we fulfil our destiny, but our fate is sealed." – **Paulo Coelho**

29. "Take chances, make mistakes. That's how you grow. Pain nourishes your courage. You have to fail in order to practice being brave." – **Mary Tyler Moore**

30. "There is no passion to be found playing small - in settling for a life that is less than the one you are capable of living."
   – Nelson Mandela

12. "You can't just fight for the money because if you do, after the first round you can think you don't need to take all the punishment; you fight for the belt plus the pride."
    – **Evander Holyfield**

13. "After climbing a great hill, one only finds that there are many more hills to climb." – **Nelson Mandela**

14. "I rewrite all the way to the printer, maybe the worst somebody would ever say of me was he was fairly undiplomatic in the way he tried to get things done, at least he tried to get things done." – **Bryant Gumbel**

15. "Courage may be the most important of all virtues because without it one cannot practice any other virtue with consistency." – **Maya Angelou**

16. "When you clench your fist, no one can put anything in your hand, nor can your hand pick up anything." – **Alex Haley**

17. "The longer you can look back the farther you can look forward." – **Winston Churchill**

18. "Everyone is more or less the master of his own fate. Our feelings are our most genuine paths to knowledge, they are chaotic, sometimes painful, sometimes contradictory, but they come from deep within us and we must key into those feelings. This is how New Visions begin." – **Al Dreadlord**

19. "To deny people their human rights is to challenge their very humanity." – **Nelson Mandela**

20. "I've always been proud to be black but proud and obsessive are different things." – **Jacob Lamar**

21. "I learned that courage was not the absence of fear, but the triumph over it. The brave man is not he who does not feel afraid, but he who conquers that fear." – **Nelson Mandela**

22. "Criticism is easy, achievement is more difficult."
    – **Winston Churchill**

CHALLENGES

1. "As long as poverty, injustice and gross inequality persist in our world, none of us can truly rest." – **Nelson Mandela**

2. "Neither the length of the struggle nor any form of severity which it may soon so make us weary or she'll make us quit." – **Winston Churchill**

3. "They probably talk about my hard childhood and never understood that all the while I was quite happy."
   – **Nikki Giovanni**

4. "Being your own man does not mean taking advantage of anyone else." – **Flip Wilson**

5. "The higher the monkey climbs the more it is exposed to danger." – **Bellas**

6. "In trouble, there are periods when I am the most attentive and thoughtful lover in the world and periods to when I am just unavailable when I surface again. I try to apply the poultice and pick up the polls I've left in relationships around me." – **Toni Cade Bambara**

7. "Many times, during auditions I was told that I couldn't carry a note with a bucket and then I still couldn't play the piano." – **Ray Charles**

8. "Yeah life hurts like hell but this is how I keep going. I have a sense of humor, I've got my brothers and sisters, I've got the ability to make something out of nothing. I can clap my hands and make magic." – **Bill T Jones**

9. "You must never make a promise which you do not fulfill."
   – **Winston Churchill**

10. "We must not become discouraged." – **Booker T Washington**

11. "To be a great Champion you must believe you are the best, if you're not pretend you are." – **Muhammad Ali**

Success

22. "Any fact facing us is not as important as our attitude toward it, for that determines our success or failure. The way you think about a fact may defeat you before you ever do anything about it. You are overcome by the fact because you think you are." – **Norman Vincent Peale**

23. "Sometimes adversity is what you need to face in order to become successful." – **Zig Ziglar**

24. "Talent alone won't make you a success. Neither will being in the right place at the right time, unless you are ready. The most important question is: 'Are you ready?'"
    – Johnny Carson

25. "Stay focused, go after your dreams and keep moving toward your goals." – **LL Cool J**

26. "I've missed more than 9000 shots in my career. I've lost almost 300 games. 26 times, I've been trusted to take the game winning shot and missed. I've failed over and over and over again in my life. And that is why I succeed."
    – Michael Jordan

27. "There is nothing wrong with dreaming big dreams, just know that all roads that lead to success have to pass through Hardwork Boulevard at some point." – **Eric Thomas**

28. "You don't have to be great to get started, but you have to get started to be great." – **Les Brown**

29. "Hold yourself responsible for a higher standard than anybody expects of you. Never excuse yourself."
    – Henry Ward Beecher

30. "When you have confidence, you can have a lot of fun. And when you have fun, you can do amazing things."
    – Joe Namath

12. "A good head and a good heart are always a formidable combination." – **Nelson Mandela**

13. "It is better to lead from behind and to put others in front, especially when you celebrate victory when nice things occur. You take the front line when there is danger. Then people will appreciate your leadership." – **Nelson Mandela**

14. "We all naturally want to become successful... we also want to take shortcuts. And it's easy to do so, but you can never take away the effort of hard work and discipline and sacrifice." – **Apolo Ohno**

15. "The will to win, the desire to succeed, the urge to reach your full potential... these are the keys that will unlock the door to personal excellence." – **Confucius**

16. "The ladder of success is more crowded at the top." – **Florence Griffith Joyner**

17. "The majority of people in the world don't do what it takes to win. Everyone is looking for the easy Road." – **Charles Barkley**

18. "Success does not consist in never making mistakes but in never making the same one a second time." – **George Bernard Shaw**

19. "Try not to become a man of success, but rather try to become a man of value." – **Albert Einstein**

20. "The most important things are the hardest things to say. They are the things you get ashamed of because words diminish your feelings - words shrink things that seem timeless when they are in your head to no more than living size when they are brought out." – **Stephen King**

21. "People of mediocre ability sometimes achieve outstanding success because they don't know when to quit. Most men succeed because they are determined to." – **George Allen, Sr.**

SUCCESS

1. "I feel that the most important requirement in success is learning to overcome failure. You must learn to tolerate it, but never accept it." – **Reggie Jackson**

2. "Nothing will work unless you do." – **Maya Angelou**

3. "Hold fast to dreams, for if dreams die life is a broken winged bird that cannot fly." – **Langston Hughes**

4. "You have seen how a man was made a slave; you shall see how a slave was made a man." – **Frederick Douglas**

5. "Free at last, Free at last, thank god almighty we are free at last." – **Dr. Martin Luther King Jr.**

6. "You will be coming through many adversities in your lifetime – negative things that can hold you back – but don't allow those situations to interfere with your journey. Stay positive, stay strong, be successful and you will, without a doubt, Make the Grade." – **Bob Lee**

7. "You must have respect for all individuals, show up when you have committed to do so, speak your mind, and always follow through on promises and or commitments."
   – **Samuel P. Peabody**

8. "If you are depressed, you are living in the past. If you are anxious, you are living in the future. If you are at peace, you are living in the present". – **Lao Tzu**

9. "Me doing the right thing has absolutely nothing to do with you doing the right thing." – **Jack Lash**

10. "Opportunities don't happen, you create them."
    – **Chris Grosser**

11. "Your assumptions are the windows on the world. Scrub them off every once in a while, or the light won't come in."
    – **Alan Alda**

24. "Loneliness expresses the pain of being alone and solitude expresses the glory of being alone." – **Paul Tillich**

25. "One of the most tragic things I know about human nature is that all of us tend to put off living. We are all dreaming of some magical rose garden over the horizon instead of enjoying the roses that are blooming outside our windows today." – **Dale Carnegie**

26. "Christmas is the spirit of giving without a thought of getting. It is happiness because we see joy in people. It is forgetting self and finding time for others. It is discarding the meaningless and stressing the true values."
    – **Thomas S. Monson**

27. "No matter how bad things are, they can always be worse. So what if my stroke left me with a speech impediment? Moses had one, and he did all right." – **Kirk Douglas**

28. "Accept responsibility for your life. Know that it is you who will get you where you want to go, no one else."
    – **Les Brown**

29. "Each of us has lived through some devastation, some loneliness, some weather superstorm or spiritual superstorm. When we look at each other we must say, I understand. I understand how you feel because I have been there myself. We must support each other because each of us is more alike than we are unalike." – **Maya Angelou**

30. "Acceptance doesn't mean resignation; it means understanding that something is what it is and that there's got to be a way through it." – **Michael J. Fox**

13. "We must use time creatively and forever realize that the time is always right to do it right." – **Martin Luther King Jr.**

14. "No one is perfect in this imperfect World."
    – **Patrice Lumumba**

15. "You can map out a fight plan or a life plan but when the action starts it may not go the way you planned and you're down to your reflexes which means your training."
    – **Joe Frazier**

16. "All my life I've had this almost Criminal optimism. I didn't care what happened. The glass was always going to be half full." – **Quincy Jones**

17. "When face-to-face with oneself there is no cop-out."
    – **Edward Kennedy Duke Ellington**

18. "And every adversity looks for the benefits that can come out of it; even bad experiences offer benefits but you have to look for them." – **Johnny Lopez**

19. "I still dream big at times but when my dreams pull apart, as they sometimes do, I don't press the panic button."
    – **Gordon Parks**

20. "Don't look back, something might be gaining on you."
    – **Leroy Satchel Paige**

21. "One cannot give to a person that which he already possesses."
    – **Toussaint l'ouverture**

22. "There is no value in life except what you choose to place upon it and no happiness in any place except what you bring to yourself." – **Henry David Thoreau**

23. "I am determined to be cheerful and happy in whatever situation I may find myself for I have learned that the greater part of our misery or unhappiness is determined not by our circumstances but by our disposition."
    – **Booker T Washington**

ACCEPTANCE

1. "Your big opportunity may be right where you are now."
   – **Napoleon Hill**

2. "We must accept finite disappointment, but never lose infinite hope." – **Martin Luther King, Jr.**

3. "Memories of our lives, of our works and our deeds will continue in others." – **Rosa Parks**

4. "I will love the light for it shows me the way, yet I will endure the darkness because it shows me the stars."
   – **Og Mandino**

5. "My sun sets to rise again?" Nice food for thought for you.
   – **Elizabeth Barrett Browning**

6. "Whatever is bringing you down, get rid of it. Because you'll find that when you're free . . . your true self comes out."
   – **Tina Turner**

7. "You can't separate peace from freedom because no one can be at peace unless he has his freedom." – **Malcolm X**

8. "How wonderful it is that nobody need wait a single moment before starting to improve the world." – **Anne Frank**

9. "Somewhere, something incredible is waiting to be known." – **Carl Sagan**

10. "Two roads diverged in a wood and I took the one less traveled by many, and that has made all the difference."
    – **Robert Frost**

11. "The meaning of life is to find your gift. The purpose of life is to give it away." – **Anonymous**

12. "Acceptance of prevailing standards often means we have no standards of our own." – **Jean Toomer**

9. "So many people get involved with carrying grudges and having these moral battles with people, where they cast themselves as the righteous and the other guy is the dirtbag. They waste tons of energy on it, create all kinds of darkness around themselves and the other person. It gets you nothing." – **Stephen J. Cannell**

10. "Any fool can criticize, condemn, and complain but it takes character and self-control to be understanding and forgiving."
– **Dale Carnegie**

FORGIVENESS

1. "We must develop and maintain the capacity to forgive. He who is devoid of the power to forgive is devoid of the power to love. There is some good in the worst of us and some evil in the best of us. When we discover this, we are less prone to hate our enemies." – **Martin Luther King, Jr**.

2. "Courageous people do not fear forgiving, for the sake of peace." – **Nelson Mandela**

3. "There is no revenge so complete as forgiveness."
   – **Josh Billings**

4. "Grudges are for those who insist that they are owed something; forgiveness, however, is for those who are substantial enough to move on." – **Criss Jami**

5. "Complaining not only ruins everybody else's day, it ruins the complainer's day, too. The more we complain, the more unhappy we get." – **Dennis Prager**

6. "We must develop and maintain the capacity to forgive. He who is devoid of the power to forgive is devoid of the power to love. There is some good in the worst of us and some evil in the best of us. When we discover this, we are less prone to hate our enemies." – **Martin Luther King, Jr.**

7. "It is wise to direct your anger towards problems - not people; to focus your energies on answers - not excuses."
   – **William Arthur Ward**

8. "A person without a sense of humor is like a wagon without springs. It's jolted by every pebble on the road."
   – **Henry Ward Beecher**

33. "I have known a vast quantity of nonsense talked about bad men not looking you in the face. Don't trust that conventional idea. Dishonesty will stare honesty out of countenance any day in the week, if there is anything to be got by it."
   – Charles Dickens

34. "I write about the power of trying, because I want to be okay with failing. I write about generosity because I battle selfishness. I write about joy because I know sorrow. I write about faith because I almost lost mine, and I know what it is to be broken and in need of redemption. I write about gratitude because I am thankful - for all of it."
   – Kristin Armstrong

35. "Whatever you want in life, other people are going to want it too. Believe in yourself enough to accept the idea that you have an equal right to it." **– Diane Sawyer**

22. "Change is the law of life. And those who look only to the past or present are certain to miss the future."
    – John F. Kennedy
23. "When we are no longer able to change a situation - we are challenged to change ourselves." **– Viktor E. Frankl**
24. "Pleasure is a shadow, wealth is vanity, and power a pageant; but knowledge is ecstatic in enjoyment, perennial in frame, unlimited in space and indefinite in duration."
    – DeWitt Clinton
25. "You've done it before and you can do it now. See the positive possibilities. Redirect the substantial energy of your frustration and turn it into positive, effective, unstoppable determination." **– Ralph Marston**
26. "There are no great limits to growth because there are no limits of human intelligence, imagination, and wonder."
    – Ronald Reagan
27. "A small group of thoughtful people could change the world. Indeed, it's the only thing that ever has." **– Margaret Mead**
28. "What lies behind us and what lies before us are tiny matters compared to what lies within us." **– Ralph Waldo Emerson**
29. "Resentment is like drinking poison and then hoping it will kill your enemies." – **Nelson Mandela**
30. "You can't start the next chapter of your life if you keep re-reading the last one." **– Unknown**
31. "A goal is not always meant to be reached, it often serves simply as something to aim at." **– Bruce Lee**
32. "Trust gives you the permission to give people direction, get everyone aligned, and give them the energy to go get the job done. Trust enables you to execute with excellence and produce extraordinary results. As you execute with excellence and deliver on your commitments, trust becomes easier to inspire, creating a flywheel of performance."
    – Douglas Conant

11. "If you respect yourself, it is easier to respect other people." – **John Singleton**

12. "There is a way to look at the past, don't hide from it; it will not catch you if you don't repeat it." – **Pearl Bailey**

13. "If you send up a weather vane or put your thumb up in the air every time you want to do something different, to find out what people are going to think about it, you're going to limit yourself. That's a very strange way to live."
    – **Jessye Norman**

14. "You want to know the secret of getting more life out of living, give, give and give… You get tenfold back when you give. If you hoard items, you get nothing in return. You're where you are today because someone gave you something to make a head start in life." – **Napoleon Hill**

15. "From what we get, we can make a living; what we give, however, makes a life." – **Arthur Ashe**

16. "I believe in living today. Not in yesterday, nor in tomorrow." – **Loretta Young**

17. "The measure of who we are is what we do with what we have." – **Vince Lombardi**

18. "People pay for what they do, and still more for what they have allowed themselves to become. And they pay for it very simply; by the lives they lead." – **James Baldwin**

19. "The question is not whether we can afford to invest in every child; it is whether we can afford not to."
    – **Marian Wright Edelman**

20. "There will always be men struggling to change, and there will always be those who are controlled by the past."
    – **Ernest J. Gaines**

21. "The walls we build around us to keep sadness out also keeps out the joy." – **Jim Rohn**

CHANGE

1. "I can't change the direction of the wind, but I can adjust my sails to always reach my destination." – **Jimmy Dean**

2. "Change your thoughts and you change your world."
   – **Norman Vincent Peale**

3. "No matter what people tell you, words and ideas can change the world" – **Robin Williams**

4. To change is to be vulnerable and to be vulnerable is to be alive. – **Alexis Davila Beaux**

5. "I hope everyone that is reading this is having a really good day. And if you are not, just know that in every new minute that passes you have an opportunity to change that."
   – **Gillian Anderson**

6. "Five years from the date of the attack that changed our world, we've come back to remember the valor of those we lost— those who innocently went to work that day and the brave souls who went in after them. We have also come to be ever mindful of the courage of those who grieve for them, and the light that still lives in their hearts." – **Rudy Giuliani**

7. "Always Do Your Best. Your best is going to change from moment to moment; it will be different when you are healthy as opposed to sick. Under any circumstance, simply do your best, and you will avoid self-judgment, self-abuse and regret."
   – **Miguel Ruiz**

8. "The man who views the world at fifty the same as he did at 20 has wasted 30 years of his life." – **Muhammad Ali**

9. "Save money and money will save you."
   – **Jamaican proverb**

10. "Do a common thing in an uncommon way."
    – **Booker T Washington**

Inspiration

32. "If future generations are to remember us more with gratitude than sorrow, we must achieve more than just the miracles of technology. We must also leave them a glimpse of the world as it was created, not just as it looked when we got through with it." **– Lyndon B. Johnson**

33. "Happiness is not something ready-made. It comes from your own actions." **– Dalai Lama**

34. "There is no exercise better for the heart than reaching down and lifting people up." **– John Holmes**

35. "What seems to be a great loss of punishment often turns out to be a blessing. I know through my own experiences that God never closes one door without opening another." **– Yolanda G Habra**

36. "But no one ever comes to you without leaving better and happier, be the living expression of God's kindness in your face, kindness in your eyes, kindness in your smile." **– Mother Teresa**

37. "Don't limit yourself. Many people limit themselves to what they think they can do. You can go as far as your mind lets you. What you believe, remember, you can achieve."
    – Mary Kay Ash

38. "Don't judge each day by the harvest you reap but by the seeds that you plant." **– Robert Louis Stevenson**

39. "Dream Big Dreams. Others May deprive you of your material wealth and cheat you in a thousand ways but no man can deprive you of the control and use of your imagination." **– Jesse Jackson**

21. "When it is obvious that the goals cannot be reached, don't adjust the goals, adjust the action steps." – **Confucius**

22. "Self-praise is for losers. Be a winner. Stand for something. Always have class, and be humble." – **John Madden**

23. "If you live to be a hundred, I want to live to be a hundred minus one day so I never have to live without you."
    – **A. A. Milne**

24. "There is nothing outside of yourself that can ever enable you to get better, stronger, richer, quicker, or smarter. Everything is within. Everything exists. Seek nothing outside of yourself." – **Miyamoto Musashi**

25. "You are the sum total of everything you've ever seen, heard, eaten, smelled, been told, forgot - it's all there. Everything influences each of us, and because of that I try to make sure that my experiences are positive." – **Maya Angelou**

26. "It's the repetition of affirmations that leads to belief. And once that belief becomes a deep conviction, things begin to happen."
    – **Muhammad Ali**

27. "Be miserable. Or motivate yourself. Whatever has to be done, it's always your choice." – **Wayne Dyer**

28. "Most folks are as happy as they make up their minds to be."
    – **Abraham Lincoln**

29. "The principles of living greatly include the capacity to face trouble with courage, disappointment with cheerfulness, and trial with humility." – **Thomas S. Monson**

30. "If you want to make peace with your enemy, you have to work with your enemy. Then he becomes your partner."
    – **Nelson Mandela**

31. "It is not true that people stop pursuing dreams because they grow old, they grow old because they stop pursuing dreams."
    – **Gabriel Garcia Marquez**

Inspiration

12. "Keep your face always toward the sunshine – and shadows will fall behind you." **– Walt Whitman**

13. "You must have a dream you believe in, with a deep passion that comes from your heart. You must be willing to have the discipline to work tirelessly, knowing that the discipline will offer you the freedom to be all that you can be in the future. Finally, you must dare to have the courage to continue when no one else believes in you. It is in these moments that you must dive deep into your spirit to believe in yourself."
 – Erline Belton

14. "I'm inspired when I walk down the street and still see people trying. A lot of them look as if they're on their last leg but they're still getting up somehow." **– Faith Ringgold**

15. "Strive to make something of yourself and strive to make the most of yourselves." **– Alexander Cromwell**

16. "We keep moving forward, opening new doors, and doing new things, because we're curious and curiosity keeps leading us down new paths." **– Walt Disney**

17. "Never be in a hurry; do everything quietly and in a calm spirit. Do not lose your inner peace for anything whatsoever, even if your whole world seems upset."
 – Saint Francis de Sales

18. "How wonderful it is that nobody need wait a single moment before starting to improve the world." **– Anne Frank**

19. "People who lack the clarity, courage, or determination to follow their own dreams will often find ways to discourage yours. Live your truth and don't EVER stop!"
 – Steve Maraboli

20. "People often say that motivation doesn't last. Well, neither does bathing. That's why we recommend it daily."
 – Zig Ziglar

121

INTEGRITY

1. "Be Impeccable with Your Word. Speak with integrity. Say only what you mean. Avoid using the word to speak against yourself or to gossip about others. Use the power of your word in the direction of truth and love." – **Miguel Ruiz**

2. "Nothing brings me more happiness than trying to help the most vulnerable people in society. It is a goal and an essential part of my life - a kind of destiny. Whoever is in distress can call on me. I will come running wherever they are."
   – Princess Diana

3. "It is of practical value to learn to like yourself. Since you must spend so much time with yourself you might as well get some satisfaction out of the relationship."
   – Norman Vincent Peale

4. "You will never be happy if you continue to search for what happiness consists of. You will never live if you are looking for the meaning of life." – **Albert Camus**

5. "Pleasure is a shadow, wealth is vanity, and power a pageant; but knowledge is ecstatic in enjoyment, perennial in frame, unlimited in space and indefinite in duration."
   – DeWitt Clinton

6. "Never be in a hurry; do everything quietly and in a calm spirit. Do not lose your inner peace for anything whatsoever, even if your whole world seems upset."
   – Saint Francis de Sales

7. "We need quiet time to examine our lives openly and honestly - spending quiet time alone gives your mind an opportunity to renew itself and create order."
   – Susan L. Taylor

8. "One of the most beautiful qualities of true friendship is to understand and to be understood."
   – **Lucius Annaeus Seneca**

9. "The two most important days in your life are the day you are born, and the day you find out why." – **Mark Twain**

10. "Some days are just bad days, that's all. You have to experience sadness to know happiness, and I remind myself that not every day is going to be a good day, that's just the way it is!" – **Dita Von Teese**

11. "Guard well within yourself that treasure, kindness. Know how to give without hesitation, how to lose without regret, how to acquire without meanness." – **George Sand**

12. "The best day of your life is the one on which you decide your life is your own. No apologies or excuses. No one to lean on, rely on, or blame. The gift is yours - it is an amazing journey - and you alone are responsible for the quality of it. This is the day your life really begins." – **Bob Moawad**

13. "It is easier to do one's duty to others than to one's self. If you do your duty to others, you are considered reliable. If you do your duty to yourself, you are considered selfish."
    – **Thomas Szasz**

14. "There are uses to adversity, and they don't reveal themselves until tested. Whether it's serious illness, financial hardship, or the simple constraint of parents who speak limited English, difficulty can tap unexpected strengths." – **Sonia Sotomayor**

15. "Sadness is a super important thing not to be ashamed about but to include in our lives. One of the bigger problems with sadness or depression is there's so much shame around it. If you have it, you're a failure." – **Mike Mills**

16. "Don't confuse poor decision-making with destiny. Own your mistakes. It's ok; we all make them. Learn from them so they can empower you!" – **Steve Maraboli**

17. "What you pay attention to grows. If your attention is attracted to negative situations and emotions, then they will grow in your awareness." – **Deepak Chopra**

18. "While you're going through this process of trying to find the satisfaction in your work, pretend you feel satisfied. Tell yourself you had a good day. Walk through the corridors with a smile rather than a scowl. Your positive energy will radiate. If you act like you're having fun, you'll find you are having fun." – **Jean Chatzky**

19. "The most important things are the hardest things to say. They are the things you get ashamed of because words diminish your feelings - words shrink things that seem timeless when they are in your head to no more than living size when they are brought out." – **Stephen King**

20. "The only person you are destined to become is the person you decide to be." – **Ralph Waldo Emerson**

21. "Don't Make Assumptions. Find the courage to ask questions and to express what you really want. Communicate with others as clearly as you can to avoid misunderstandings, sadness and drama. With just this one agreement, you can completely transform your life." – **Miguel Ruiz**

22. "Let me define a leader. He must have vision and passion and not be afraid of any problem. Instead, he should know how to defeat it. Most importantly, he must work with integrity." – **A. P. J. Abdul Kalam**

23. "Achievement of your happiness is the only moral purpose of your life, and that happiness, not pain or mindless self-indulgence, is the proof of your moral integrity, since it is the proof and the result of your loyalty to the achievement of your values." – **Ayn Rand**

24. "Words are singularly the most powerful force available to humanity. We can choose to use this force constructively with words of encouragement, or destructively using words of despair. Words have energy and power with the ability to help, to heal, to hinder, to hurt, to harm, to humiliate and to humble." – **Yehuda Berg**

25. "There are no great limits to growth because there are no limits of human intelligence, imagination, and wonder."
    – **Ronald Reagan**

26. "Far and away the best prize that life has to offer is the chance to work hard at work worth doing."
    – **Theodore Roosevelt**

27. "The price tag you put on yourself decides your worth. Underestimating yourself will cost you dearly."
    – **Apoorve Dubey**

28. "No man will make a great leader who wants to do it all himself or get all the credit for doing it."
    – **Andrew Carnegie**

29. "The problem with thick skin is that it leaves you impervious to the sharpest of pins. Everything becomes dull. But without that sense of pain, there cannot be that sense of relief. Ultimately, the thickened skin leaves you numb, incapable of feeling the highs and lows of life. It leaves you rough like a rock and just as inanimate." – **Michael Soll**

30. "You have enemies? Good. That means you've stood up for something, sometime in your life." – **Winston Churchill**

31. "When they go low we go high." – **Michelle Obama**

32. "Appreciation is a wonderful thing: It makes what is excellent in others belong to us as well." – **Voltaire**

33. "The happiness of your life depends upon the quality of your thoughts: therefore, guard accordingly, and take care that you entertain no notions unsuitable to virtue and reasonable nature." – **Marcus Aurelius**

34. "When you really listen to another person from their point of view, and reflect back to them that understanding, it's like giving them emotional oxygen." – **Stephen Covey**

LOVE AND FRIENDSHIP

Bob Marley stated: "Only once in your life, I truly believe, you find someone who can completely turn your world around. You tell them things that you've never shared with another soul and they absorb everything you say and actually want to hear more. You share hopes for the future, dreams that will never come true, goals that were never achieved and the many disappointments life has thrown at you. When something wonderful happens, you can't wait to tell them about it, knowing they will share in your excitement. They are not embarrassed to cry with you when you are hurting or laugh with you when you make a fool of yourself. Never do they hurt your feelings or make you feel like you are not good enough, but rather they build you up and show you the things about yourself that make you special and even beautiful. There is never any pressure, jealousy or competition but only a quiet calmness when they are around. You can be yourself and not worry about what they will think of you because they love you for who you are.

The things that seem insignificant to most people such as a note, song or walk become invaluable treasures kept safe in your heart to cherish forever. Memories of your childhood come back and are so clear and vivid it's like being young again. Colors seem brighter and more brilliant. Laughter seems part of daily life where before it was infrequent or didn't exist at all. A phone call or two during the day helps to get you through a long day's work and always brings a smile to your face. In their presence, there's no need for continuous conversation, but you find you're quite content in just having them nearby. Things that never interested you before become fascinating because you know they are important to this person who is so special to you. You think of this person on every occasion and in everything you do. Simple things bring them to mind like a pale blue sky, gentle wind or even a storm cloud on the horizon. You open your heart knowing that there's a chance it may be broken one day and in opening your heart, you experience a love and joy that you never dreamed possible. You find that being vulnerable is the only way to allow your heart to feel true pleasure that's so real it scares you. You find strength in knowing you have a true friend and possibly a soul mate who will remain loyal to the end. Life seems completely different, exciting and worthwhile. Your only hope and security is in knowing that they are a part of your life."

1. "Being deeply loved by someone gives you strength, while loving someone deeply gives you courage." – **Lao Tzu**

2. "Sometimes the heart sees what is invisible to the eye." – **H. Jackson Brown, Jr**.

3. "Do all things with love." – **Og Mandino**

4. "The first duty of love is to listen." – **Paul Tillich**

5. "We waste time looking for the perfect lover, instead of creating the perfect love." – **Tom Robbins**

6. "And now these three remain: faith, hope, and love. But the greatest of these is love." – **1 Corinthians 13:13**

7. "Love does not consist of gazing at each other, but in looking outward together in the same direction." – **Antoine de Saint-Exupery**

8. "A loving heart is the truest wisdom." – **Charles Dickens**

9. "The most precious gift we can offer anyone is our attention. When mindfulness embraces those we love, they will bloom like flowers." – **Thich Nhat Hanh**

10. "Loves takes off masks that we fear we cannot live without and know we cannot live within." – **James Baldwin**

11. "You know you're in love when you don't want to fall asleep because reality is finally better than your dreams." – **Dr. Seuss**

12. "It is not a lack of love, but a lack of friendship that makes unhappy marriages." – **Friedrich Nietzsche**

13. "Where there is love, there is life." – **Mahatma Gandhi**

14. "Let love and faithfulness never leave you; bind them around your neck, write them on the tablet of your heart." – **Proverbs 3:3**

15. "Love is a fruit in season at all times, and within reach of every hand." – **Mother Teresa**

16. "The best and most beautiful things in this world cannot be seen or even heard, but must be felt with the heart."
    – **Helen Keller**

17. "Love is not a matter of counting the years... but making the years count." – **Michelle Amand**

18. "Love recognizes no barriers. It jumps hurdles, leaps fences, penetrates walls to arrive at its destination full of hope." – **Maya Angelou**

19. "You come to love not by finding the perfect person, but by learning to see an imperfect person perfectly." – **Sam Keen**

20. "Do everything in love." – **1 Corinthians 16:14**

21. "Darkness cannot drive out darkness; only light can do that. Hate cannot drive out hate; only love can do that."
    – **Dr. Martin Luther King Jr.**

22. "Let my soul smile through my heart and my heart smile through my eyes, that I may scatter rich smiles in sad hearts." – **Paramahansa Yogananda**

23. "Somewhere we know that without silence words lose their meaning, that without listening speaking no longer heals, that without distance closeness cannot cure." – **Henri Nouwen**

24. "The best way to find out if you can trust somebody is to trust them." – **Ernest Hemingway**

25. "Do not think that love in order to be genuine has to be extraordinary. What we need is to love without getting tired. Be faithful in small things because it is in them that your strength lies." – **Mother Teresa**

26. "I am determined to be cheerful and happy in whatever situation I may find myself. For I have learned that the greater part of our misery or unhappiness is determined not by our circumstance but by our disposition."
    – **Martha Washington**

27. "We write for the same reason that we walk, talk, climb mountains or swim the oceans - because we can. We have some impulse within us that makes us want to explain ourselves to other human beings. That's why we paint, that's why we dare to love someone - because we have the impulse to explain who we are." – **Maya Angelou**

28. "A moment of anger can destroy a lifetime of work, whereas a moment of love can break barriers that took a lifetime to build." – **Leon Brown**

29. "Grief can be the garden of compassion. If you keep your heart open through everything, your pain can become your greatest ally in your life's search for love and wisdom."
    – **Rumi**

30. "If you're going to be sick and not sure about the future of your life, it's pretty nice to have someone who loves you."
    – **Sammy Davis Jr**.

31. "I am convinced that material things can contribute a lot to making one's life pleasant, but, basically, if you do not have very good friends and relatives who matter to you, life will be really empty and sad and material things cease to be important." – **David Rockefeller**

32. "Love one another and help others to rise to the higher levels, simply by pouring out love. Love is infectious and the greatest healing energy." – **Sai Baba**

33. "To let friendship die away by negligence and silence is certainly not wise. It is voluntarily to throw away one of the greatest comforts of this weary pilgrimage."
   – **Samuel Johnson**

34. "If two friends ask you to judge a dispute, don't accept, because you will lose one friend; on the other hand, if two strangers come with the same request, accept because you will gain one friend." – **Saint Augustine**

35. "When we honestly ask ourselves which person in our lives means the most to us, we often find that it is those who, instead of giving advice, solutions, or cures, have chosen rather to share our pain and touch our wounds with a warm and tender hand." – **Henri Nouwen**

36. "Kindness is in our power, even when fondness is not."
   – **Samuel Johnson**

37. "Old friends pass away, new friends appear. It is just like the days. An old day passes, a new day arrives. The important thing is to make it meaningful: a meaningful friend - or a meaningful day." – **Dalai Lama**

38. "Spread love everywhere you go. Let no one ever come to you without leaving happier." – **Mother Teresa**

39. "Walking with a friend in the dark is better than walking alone in the light." – **Helen Keller**

40. "Remember that the most valuable antiques are dear old friends." – **H. Jackson Brown, Jr.**

41. "The bond that links your true family is not one of blood, but of respect and joy in each other's life." – **Richard Bach**

42. "Don't walk behind me; I may not lead. Don't walk in front of me; I may not follow. Just walk beside me and be my friend." – **Albert Camus**

43. "Cherish your human connections - your relationships with friends and family." – **Barbara Bush**

44. "Treat others as you wish to be treated. Don't just be nice, but be kind to other people. That can be so rewarding." – **Mary Lambert**

45. "Whatever we are waiting for - peace of mind, contentment, grace, the inner awareness of simple abundance - it will surely come to us, but only when we are ready to receive it with an open and grateful heart." – **Sarah Ban Breathnach**

46. "We've got this gift of love, but love is like a precious plant. You can't just accept it and leave it in the cupboard or just think it's going to get on by itself. You've got to keep watering it. You've got to really look after it and nurture it." – **John Lennon**

47. "At times, our own light goes out and is rekindled by a spark from another person. Each of us has cause to think with deep gratitude of those who have lighted the flame within us." – **Albert Schweitzer**

48. "Happiness is not a brilliant climax to years of grim struggle and anxiety. It is a long succession of little decisions simply to be happy in the moment." – **J. Donald Walters**

49. "If instead of a gem, or even a flower, we should cast the gift of a loving thought into the heart of a friend, that would be giving as the angels give." – **George MacDonald**

50. "No act of kindness, no matter how small, is ever wasted." – **Aesop**

PART THREE

DOCTOR BOB'S TOP 120 FAN FAVE QUOTES

Most of the Celebrities That We Recognize Have a Strong Opinion or Quote About Something They Have Accomplished, Enjoy or Believe In… Here Are 120 of Those Fan Favorite Quotes

Your Daily Dose of Quotes and Anecdotes

DOCTOR BOB'S TOP 120 FAN FAVE QUOTES

1. "I don't really think it'll ever be enough. I used to equate success with my finances because I didn't have anything, and when you don't have any money, it seems money is the answer to all your problems. Then you get money, and you realize that you've got a whole new set of problems." – **50 Cent**

2. "Sometimes you have to allow yourself to be sad in order to move forward." – **Adele**

3. "You have to love what you do to want to do it every day." – **Aaliyah**

4. "It's much more interesting to embrace who you really are rather than waste energy pretending to be someone else." – **Adam Levine**

5. "It's easy to fool the eye but it's hard to fool the heart." – **Al Pacino**

6. "I'd rather not have anything than be a liar." – **Alicia Keys**

7. "Be ready for when your time comes, you will have that window of opportunity, so seize the moment and capitalize on it." – **Anthony Anderson**

8. "Be happy with being you. Love your flaws. Own your quirks. And know that you are just as perfect as anyone else, exactly as you are." – **Ariana Grande**

9. "The reality is, some people don't want you to change or go anywhere different." – **Babyface**

10. "I get nervous when I don't get nervous...If I'm nervous I know I'm going to have a good show." – **Beyoncé Knowles**

11. "To be still standing 20 years in this business is a great feeling,.. I can't even tell you." – **Blair Underwood**

12. "I want to stand for something, and it's probably going to be something that some people stand against." – **Blake Shelton**

13. "I feel that the simplicity of life is just being yourself." – **Bobby Brown**

14. "You must lose everything in order to gain anything." – **Brad Pitt**

15. "It may not be the best in someone else's eyes, but it's the best I can do." – **Brandy Norwood**

16. "Be in control. Know who you are. And don't try to be different just to be different." – **Bruno Mars**

17. "Every day is a new day, and you'll never be able to find happiness if you don't move on." – **Carrie Underwood**

18. "Haters keep on hating, cause somebody's gotta do it." – **Chris Brown**

19. "The roughest road often leads to the top." – **Christina Aguilera**

20. "The impact of a conscious artist is necessary, and it ripples through the world." – **Common**

21. "Every group has its idiosyncrasies, but at a certain point we all are human." – **D. L. Hughley**

22. "Nobody can stop you but you. And shame on you if you're the one who stops yourself." – **Damon Wayans**

23. "I don't know where I'm going from here, but I promise it won't be boring." – **David Bowie**

24. "But out of limitations comes creativity." – **Debbie Allen**

25. "I say luck is when an opportunity comes along and you're prepared for it." – **Denzel Washington**

26. "You know, you do need mentors, but in the end, you really just need to believe in yourself." – **Diana Ross**

27. "It's not hard to keep up the image we chose. It's not hard to stay yourselves." – **Donnie Wahlberg**

28. "No matter how hard you work to bring yourself up, there's someone out there working just as hard, to put you down...."
 – **Dr. Dre**

29. "Sometimes it's the journey that teaches you a lot about your destination." – **Drake**

30. "With drive and a bit of talent, you can move mountains."
 – **Dwayne Johnson**

31. "A lot of truth is said in jest." – **Eminem**

32. "I think that you make the best choice with the information that you have before you at that given time." – **Eriq La Salle**

33. "The music business is motivated by money. Music is motivated by energy and feelings." – **Erykah Badu**

34. "My lips are big, but my talent is bigger."
 – **Fantasia Barrino**

35. "If I do look back, I'll say that I'm blessed. I'm blessed, and I appreciate God for not only letting me live through everything, but to prosper." – **Flavor Flav**

36. "I've always known, before I had a record deal, that the thing is to go out and put on the show. I've been doing that from day one." – **Flo-Rida**

37. "Stereotypes do exist, but we have to walk through them."
 – **Forest Whitaker**

38. "Sometimes the best things are right in front of you; it just takes some time to see them." – **Gladys Knight**

39. "I live my life, because I dare. I dare to show up when everyone else might hide their faces and hide their bodies in shame." – **Gabourey Sidibe**

40. "I'm not going to change the world overnight."
 – **Gabrielle Union**

41. "We can even sing off key, but if it's produced properly it can be a hit." – **Grandmaster Flash**

42. "Sometimes you have to sacrifice your performance for high heels." – **Gwen Stefani**

43. "Beauty, to me, is about being comfortable in your own skin. That, or a kick-ass red lipstick." – **Gwyneth Paltrow**

44. "I think it's always best to be who you are." – **Halle Berry**

45. "We must stop thinking of the individual and start thinking about what is best for society." – **Hillary Clinton**

46. "You don't have to hold on to the pain, to hold on to the memory." – **Janet Jackson**

47. "Be very nervous of the shaky hands." – **Ja Rule**

48. "We all think there is a formula, (but) as long as we love our children, that's really the only solid thing I know that works across the board." – **Jada Pinkett Smith**

49. "In our music, in our everyday life, there are so many negative things. Why not have something positive and stamp it with blackness?" – **Jamie Foxx**

50. "I'm far from being god, but I work god damn hard." – **Jay Z**

51. "You have to accept the plan and realize that if you slip, and you might, you can't use that as a reason to give up or stop." – **Jennifer Hudson**

52. "I judge people on how they smell, not how they look." – **Jennifer Lopez**

53. "Listening is more important than talking. Just hit your mark and believe what you say. Just listen to people and react to what they are saying." – **Jimmy Fallon**

54. "You learn so much from taking chances, whether they work out or not. Either way, you can grow from the experience and become stronger and smarter." – **John Legend**

55. "There really is no weight to telling the truth. It's a little scary sometimes, but if you tell the truth, you don't have to be looking over your shoulder." – **Jussie Smollet**

56. "Friends are the best to turn to when you're having a rough day." – **Justin Bieber**

57. "There's nothing wrong with shooting for the stars." – **Justin Timberlake**

58. "Nothing in life is promised except death." – **Kanye West**

59. "You can't stop loving or wanting to love because when its right it's the best thing in the world." – **Keith Sweat**

60. "I don't want to impress, I want to inspire." – **Keith Urban**

61. "Learn to embrace your own unique beauty, celebrate your unique gifts with confidence. Your imperfections are actually a gift." – **Kerri Washington**

62. "Life is too short to worry about what others say about you. Have fun and give them something to talk about." – **Kevin Hart**

63. "Don't you ever let a soul in the world tell you that you can't be exactly who you are." – **Lady Gaga**

64. "Everything we do should be a result of our gratitude for what God has done for us." – **Lauryn Hill**

65. "To all the positions, I just bring the determination to win." – **LeBron James**

66. "It's very important to vote. People died for this right." – **Lenny Kravitz**

67. "I think when you move past your fear and you go after your dreams wholeheartedly, you become free." - **LL Cool J**

68. "Greatness comes from fear. Fear can either shut us down and we go home, or we fight through it." – **Lionel Richie**

69. "I just always expect the best because I'm a competitor and if I'm competing, then obviously I'm trying to be better in everything." – **Lil Wayne**

70. "All kids need is a little help, a little hope and somebody who believes in them." – **Magic Johnson**

71. "I don't think anyone knows as much about what's right for me as I do." – **Mariah Carey**

72. "The quality, not the longevity, of one's life is what is important." – **Martin Luther King, Jr.**

73. "If you want something to work, if it means that much to you; KEEP IT TO YOURSELF." – **Michael Ealy**

74. "The meaning of life is contained in every single expression of life." – **Michael Jackson**

75. "You have to expect things of yourself before you can do them." - **Michael Jordan**

76. "If you believe in yourself anything is possible." – **Miley Cyrus**

77. "You have to be ready to sing and perform at any time." – **Missy Elliot**

78. "Learning how to be still, to really be still and let life happen - that stillness becomes a radiance." – **Morgan Freeman**

79. "I'm getting to the point where they see me as a good actor, rather than just a good guy who can act." – **Morris Chestnut**

80. "I make a lot of money and I'm worth every cent." – **Naomi Campbell**

81. "To be compared to Will Smith is probably one of the coolest things because that's who I came up admiring." – **Nick Cannon**

82. "You should never feel bad about yourself because the trend everyone is wearing doesn't fit you" – **Nicole Richie**

83. "True confidence leaves no room for jealousy. When you know you are great, you have no need to hate."
    – **Nikki Minaj**

84. "The more you praise and celebrate your life, the more there is in life to celebrate." – **Oprah Winfrey**

85. "The way I see it, you should live everyday like it's your birthday." – **Paris Hilton**

86. "Compassion is an action word with no boundaries."– **Prince**

87. "If you dream and you believe, you can do it." – **Puff Daddy**

88. "Don't you want to know what's real and what's not?" – **Queen Latifah**

89. "They say marriage will change you but it didn't change me. Being in love changed me." – **R. Kelly**

90. "As a young female, I think it's important that young people know there's nothing wrong with having fun, nobody is telling us to be square or be boring, but we have to be safe."
    - – **Rihanna**

91. "You'll have time to rest when you're dead."
    – **Robert De Niro**

92. "Memories of our lives, of our works and our deeds will continue in others." – **Rosa Parks**

93. "If you have an opportunity to use your voice you should use it." – **Samuel L. Jackson**

94. "I realize everybody wants what they don't have. But at the end of the day, what you have inside is much more beautiful than what's on the outside!" – **Selena Gomez**

95. "Family's first, and that's what matters most. We realize that our love goes deeper than the tennis game."
    – **Serena Williams**

96. "Everything happens for a reason. I'm used to it, I prepare for it." – **Shaquille O'Neal**

97. "My attitude is, if someone's going to criticize me, tell me to my face." – **Simon Cowell**

98. "We're all going to be victims of temptation at several points in our lives." – **Smokey Robinson**

99. "If it's flipping hamburgers at McDonald's, be the best hamburger flipper in the world. Whatever it is you do you have to master your craft." – **Snoop Dogg**

100. "Any decision I make is based on myself, and the only person I have to give an explanation to is God."
– **Solange Knowles**

101. "I think it is very important that films make people look at what they've forgotten." – **Spike Lee**

102. "I don't want to be 60 years old standing on stage telling some jokes. I want my life to mean something."
– **Steve Harvey**

103. "You can't base your life on other people's expectations."
– **Stevie Wonder**

104. "Beauty is everything and beauty is within, however, if you don't feel good on the outside, then you will not look good."
– **Tamar Braxton**

105. "Use missteps as stepping stones to deeper understanding and greater achievement." – **Susan Taylor**

106. "I don't harp on the negative because if you do, then there's no progression. There's no forward movement. You got to always look on the bright side of things, and we are in control. Like, you have control over the choices you make."
– **Taraji P. Henson**

107. "I am an over-achiever, and I want to be known for the good things in my life." - **Taylor Swift**

108. "My future's about trying to be a better man."
 – **Terrence Howard**

109. "I always look for a challenge and something that's different." – **Tom Cruise**

110. "To do what you love can sometimes be stressful."
 – **Toni Braxton**

111. "We need to pay attention to each other. We are our brother's keepers. We are our sister's keepers." – **Trai Byers**

112. "I'm a reflection of the community." – **Tupac Shakur**

113. "I'm competitive with myself. I always try to push past my own borders." – **Tyra Banks**

114. "Strivers achieve what dreamers believe." – **Usher Raymond**

115. "Success is the sweetest revenge." – **Vanessa Williams**

116. "A great figure or physique is nice, but it's self-confidence that makes someone really sexy." – **Vivica Fox**

117. "What drives the creative person is that we see it all."
 – **Wanda Sykes**

118. "God gave me a voice to sing with, and when you have that, what other gimmick is there?" – **Whitney Houston**

119. "I am where I am because I believe in all possibilities."
 – **Whoopi Goldberg**

120. "I don't know what my calling is, but I want to be here for a bigger reason. I strive to be like the greatest people who have ever lived." – **Will Smith**

Your Daily Dose of Quotes and Anecdotes

JUST FOR FUN...
15 MEMORABLE MOVIE LINES

1. "Go ahead, make my day." – **Sudden Impact**
2. "May the Force be with you." – **Star Wars**
3. "Love means never having to say you're sorry." – **Love Story**
4. "The stuff that dreams are made of." – **The Maltese Falcon**
5. "E.T. phone home." – **E.T. The Extra-Terrestrial**
6. "There's no place like home." – **The Wizard of Oz**
7. "Show me the money!" – **Jerry Maguire**
8. "After all, tomorrow is another day!" – **Gone with the Wind**
9. "Today, I consider myself the luckiest man on the face of the earth." – **The Pride of the Yankees**
10. "Mama always said life was like a box of chocolates. You never know what you're gonna get." – **Forrest Gump**
11. "Well, nobody's perfect." – **Some Like It Hot**
12. "Wait a minute, wait a minute. You ain't heard nothin' yet!" – **The Jazz Singer**
13. "I have always depended on the kindness of strangers." – **A Streetcar Named Desire**
14. "Hasta la vista, baby." – **Terminator 2: Judgment Day**
15. "I'm king of the world!" – **Titanic**

QUOTES MEANT TO MOTIVATE YOU

1. "There's always something to suggest that you'll never be who you wanted to be. Your choice is to take it or keep on moving."
   - Phylicia Rashad

2. "I have learned over the years that when one's mind is made up, this diminishes fear; knowing what must be done does away with fear." **- Rosa Parks**

3. "The kind of beauty I want most is the hard-to-get kind that comes from within — strength, courage, dignity."
   - Ruby Dee

4. "As you become more clear about who you are, you'll be better able to decide what is best for you — the first time around." **- Oprah**

5. "A woman needs someone she can trust, someone who laughs when she laughs, but who has different ideas, so she can learn from and teach to them. She needs someone who will stand up with her and encourage her to be a woman—not just a female. See where you are, admit what you know, and what you need, and search for a sister friend."
   - Maya Angelou

6. "Our mistreatment was just not right, and I was tired of it."
   – Rosa Parks

7. "Injustice anywhere is a threat to justice everywhere."
   – Martin Luther King, Jr.

8. "If you succumb to the temptation of using violence in the struggle, unborn generations will be the recipients of a long and desolate night of bitterness, and your chief legacy to the future will be an endless reign of meaningless chaos."
   – Martin Luther King, Jr.

9. "The first step toward success is taken when you refuse to be a captive of the environment in which you first find yourself." – **Mark Caine**

10. "There are two kinds of opportunities: one which we chance upon, the other which we create." – **Ruth Benedict**

11. "If your heart's attached to it, then your mind will be attached to it. When you have a passion for something, then you tend not only to be better at it, but you work harder at it too." – **Vera Wang**

12. "Courage is only the accumulation of small steps."
    – **George Konrad**

13. "Learn from the mistakes of others. You can't live long enough to make them all yourself." – **Eleanor Roosevelt**

14. "Life is trying things to see if they work." – **Ray Bradbury**

15. "Don't let life discourage you. Everyone who got where he is had to begin where he was." – **Richard L. Evans**

16. "Am I not destroying my enemies when I make friends of them?" – **Abraham Lincoln**

17. "If you don't go after what you want, you'll never have it. If you don't ask, the answer is always no. If you don't step forward, you are always in the same place." – **Nora Roberts**

18. "Breathe. Let go. And remind yourself that this very moment is the only one you know you have for sure."
    – **Oprah Winfrey**

19. "Don't let the fear of the time it will take to accomplish something stand in the way of your doing it. The time will pass anyway; we might just as well put that passing time to the best possible us." – **Earl Nightingale**

20. "Most of the important things in the world have been accomplished by people who have kept on trying when there seemed to be no help at all." – **Dale Carnegie**

21. "Good actions give strength to ourselves and inspire good actions in others." — **Plato**

QUOTES TO HELP KEEP YOU ON COURSE

1. "Racism is not an excuse to not do the best you can."
   - Arthur Ashe

2. "Life is short, and it's up to you to make it sweet."
   - Sadie Delany

3. "Success is most often achieved by those who don't know that failure is inevitable." – **Coco Chanel**

4. "I refuse to accept other people's ideas of happiness for me. As if there's a one size fits all standard for happiness." – **Kanye West**

5. "There is only one way to avoid criticism: do nothing, say nothing, and be nothing." – **Aristotle**

6. "When I let go of what I am, I become what I might be." –**Lao Tzu**

7. "I am thankful for all of those who said NO to me. It's because of them I'm doing it myself." – **Albert Einstein**

8. "Only those who will risk going too far can possibly find out how far one can go." – **T. S. Eliot**

9. "Only those who play to win. Only those who risk to win. History favors risk-takers. Forgets the timid. Everything else is commentary." – **Iveta Cherneva**

10. "I always did something I was a little not ready to do. I think that's how you grow. When there's that moment of Wow, I'm not really sure I can do this, and you push through those moments, that's when you have a breakthrough." – **Marissa Mayer**

11. "If you don't build your dream, someone else will hire you to help them build theirs." – **Dhirubhai Ambani**

12. "Don't be too timid and squeamish about your actions. All life is an experiment. The more experiments you make the better." - **Ralph Waldo Emerson**

13. "And the day came when the risk to remain tight in a bud was more painful than the risk it took to blossom." – **Anais Nin**

14. "Life is being on the wire, everything else is just waiting." – **Karl Wallenda**

15. "Pearls don't lie on the seashore. If you want one, you must dive for it." – **Chinese proverb**

QUOTES THAT CHALLENGE YOUR POWER WITHIN

1. "Passion is energy. Feel the power that comes from focusing on what excites you." - **Oprah Winfrey**

2. "I had to make my own living and my own opportunity. But I made it! Don't sit down and wait for the opportunities to come. Get up and make them." - **Madam C.J. Walker**

3. "Belief in oneself and knowing who you are, I mean, that's the foundation for everything great." - **Jay-Z**

4. "Many people don't focus enough on execution. If you make a commitment to get something done, you need to follow through on that commitment." - **Kenneth Chenault**

5. "If everything was perfect, you would never learn, and you would never grow." - **Beyoncé Knowles**

6. "If you wake up deciding what you want to give versus what you're going to get, you become a more successful person. In other words, if you want to make money, you have to help someone else make money." - **Russell Simmons**

7. "People from all walks of life and all over the world look at me and know my humble beginnings and know that everything I've done has been through hard work. People respect me as a marketer and brand builder." - **Sean Combs**

8. "I want to stop transforming and just start being."
   - **Ursula Burns**

9. "I built a conglomerate and emerged the richest black man in the world in 2008 but it didn't happen overnight. It took me 30 years to get to where I am today. Youths of today aspire to be like me but they want to achieve it overnight. It's not going to work. To build a successful business, you must start

small and dream big. In the journey of entrepreneurship, tenacity of purpose is supreme." - **Aliko Dangote**

10. "History has always been a series of pendulum swings, but the individual doesn't have to get caught in that."
    - Robert L. Johnson

11. "One of the challenges associated with a company becoming large is that companies become hierarchical. They become bureaucratic. They become slow. They become risk averse."
    - Kenneth C. Frazier

12. "You can and should set your own limits and clearly articulate them. This takes courage, but it is also liberating and empowering, and often earns you new respect."
    - Rosalind Brewer

13. "Keep going. No matter what." - **Reginald Lewis**

14. "Hold on to your dreams of a better life and stay committed to striving to realize it."- **Earl G. Graves, Sr.**

15. "You are where you are today because you stand on somebody's shoulders. And wherever you are heading, you cannot get there by yourself. If you stand on the shoulders of others, you have a reciprocal responsibility to live your life so that others may stand on your shoulders. It's the quid pro quo of life. We exist temporarily through what we take, but we live forever through what we give." - **Vernon Jordan**

16. "I have this ability to find this hidden talent in people that sometimes even they didn't know they had." - **Berry Gordy**

17. "The road back may not be as short as we wish... But there are solid reasons to feel confident about the future."
    - Richard Parsons

18. "My Vocation is my Vacation. I love what I do."
    - **Nick Cannon**

19. "There is nothing a woman can't do. Men might think they do things all by themselves but a woman is always there guiding them or helping them." - **Marjorie Joyner**

20. "When I was younger there was something in me. I had passion. I may not have known what I was going to do with that passion, but there was something - and I still feel it. It's this little engine that roars inside of me and I just want to keep going and going." - **Sheila Johnson**

21. "Self-love has very little to do with how you feel about your outer self. It's about accepting all of yourself." - **Tyra Banks**

22. "You have to remember that the hard days are what make you stronger. The bad days make you realize what a good day is. If you never had any bad days, you would never have that sense of accomplishment." – **Aly Rais**man

23. "All the great things are simple, and many can be expressed in a single word: freedom, justice, honor, duty, mercy, hope." – **Winston Churchill**

24. "Between stimulus and response, there is a space. In that space is our power to choose our response. In our response lies our growth and our freedom." – **Viktor E. Frankl**

25. "Great men are like eagles and build their nest on some lofty solitude." – **Arthur Schopenhauer**

26. "Logic will get you from A to Z. Imagination will get you everywhere." – **Albert Einstein**

QUOTES THAT CREATE AWARENESS

1. "Life is short, and it's up to you to make it sweet."
   – **Sadie Delany**

2. "Defining myself, as opposed to being defined by others, is one of the most difficult challenges I face."
   – **Carol Moseley-Braun**

3. "Sometimes, I feel discriminated against, but it does not make me angry. It merely astonishes me. How can any deny themselves the pleasure of my company? It's beyond me."
   – **Zora Neale Hurston**

4. "I will not have my life narrowed down. I will not bow down to somebody else's whim or to someone else's ignorance."
   – **bell hooks**

5. "Don't wait around for other people to be happy for you. Any happiness you get you've got to make yourself."
   – **Alice Walker**

6. "In every crisis there is a message. Crises are nature's way of forcing change — breaking down old structures, shaking loose negative habits so that something new and better can take their place." — **Susan L. Taylor**

7. "No person is your friend who demands your silence, or denies your right to grow. " – **Alice Walker**

8. "All the money in the world doesn't mean a thing if you don't have time to enjoy it." – **Oprah Winfrey**

9. "Deal with yourself as an individual worthy of respect and make everyone else deal with you the same way."
   – **Nikki Giovanni**

10. "Trust yourself. Think for yourself. Act for yourself. Speak for yourself. Be yourself. Imitation is suicide."
    – **Marva Collins**

11. "I define joy as a sustained sense of well-being and internal peace – a connection to what matters." – **Oprah Winfrey**

12. "I think there are things for all of us to do as long as we're here and we're healthy." – **Gwendolyn Brooks**

13. "If you don't understand yourself you don't understand anybody else." – **Nikki Giovanni**

14. "A crown, if it hurts us, is not worth wearing."
    – **Pearl Bailey**

15. "Give light and people will find the way." – **Ella Baker**

16. "Self-esteem means knowing you are the dream."
    – **Oprah Winfrey**

17. "Take responsibility for yourself because no one's going to take responsibility for you. I'm not a victim. I grow from this and I learn." – **Tyra Banks**

18. "Surround yourself with only people who are going to lift you higher." – **Oprah Winfrey**

19. "The times may have changed, but the people are still the same. We're still looking for love, and that will always be our struggle as human beings." – **Halle Berry**

20. "Once we recognize what it is we are feeling, once we recognize we can feel deeply, love deeply, can feel joy, then we will demand that all parts of our lives produce that kind of joy." – **Audre Lorde**

21. "Whatever someone did to you in the past has no power over the present. Only you give it power." — **Oprah Winfrey**

22. "Winning is great, sure, but if you are really going to do something in life, the secret is learning how to lose. Nobody goes undefeated all the time. If you can pick up after a crushing defeat, and go on to win again, you are going to be a champion someday." – **Wilma Rudolph**

23. "You may encounter many defeats, but you must not be defeated. In fact, it may be necessary to encounter the defeats, so you can know who you are, what you can rise from, how you can still come out of it." – **Maya Angelou**

24. "I didn't have anybody, really, no foundation in life, so I had to make my own way. Always, from the start. I had to go out in the world and become strong, to discover my mission in life." – **Tina Turner**

25. "Think like a queen. A queen is not afraid to fail. Failure is another steppingstone to greatness." – **Oprah Winfrey**

QUOTES THAT MAKE YOU THINK TWICE

1. "It's time for you to move, realizing that the thing you are seeking is also seeking you." – **Iyanla Vanzant**

2. "You are on the eve of a complete victory. You can't go wrong. The world is behind you." – **Josephine Baker**

3. "You can fall, but you can rise also." – **Angelique Kidjo**

4. "You will be wounded many times in your life. You'll make mistakes. Some people will call them failures, but I have learned that failure is really God's way of saying, "Excuse me, you're moving in the wrong direction." It's just an experience, just an experience." – **Oprah Winfrey**

5. "The triumph can't be had without the struggle."
   – **Wilma Rudolph**

6. "We will be ourselves and live free, or die in the attempt. Harriet Tubman was not our great-grandmother for nothing." – **Alice Walker**

7. "It's a long old road, but I know I'm gonna find the end." – **Bessie Smith**

8. "'I can't' are two words that have never been in my vocabulary. I believe in me more than anything in this world." – **Wilma Rudolph**

9. "Someone was hurt before you, wronged before you, hungry before you, frightened before you, beaten before you, humiliated before you, raped before you…yet, someone survived…You can do anything you choose to do."
   – **Maya Angelou**

10. "When I dare to be powerful – to use my strength in the service of my vision, then it becomes less and less important whether I am afraid." – **Audre Lorde**

11. "Fear is a disease that eats away at logic and makes man inhuman." – **Marian Anderson**

12. "When there is no enemy within, the enemies outside cannot hurt you." – **African Proverb**

13. "Whatever you fear most has no power – it is your fear that has the power. The thing itself cannot touch you. But if you allow your fear to seep into your mind and overtake your thoughts, it will rob you of your life." – **Oprah Winfrey**

14. "When we drop fear, we can draw nearer to people, we can draw nearer to the earth, we can draw nearer to all the heavenly creatures that surround us." — **bell hooks**

15. "No person has the right to rain on your dreams."
 – **Marian Wright Edelman**

16. "Success doesn't come to you…you go to it." – **Marva Collins**

17. "Doing the best at this moment puts you in the best place for the next moment." - **Oprah Winfrey**

18. "The thing that makes you exceptional, if you are at all, is inevitably that which must also make you lonely."
 – **Lorraine Hansberry**

19. "You are the designer of your destiny; you are the author of your story." - **Lisa Nichols**

20. "Whatever we believe about ourselves and our ability comes true for us." – **Susan L. Taylor**

21. "It isn't where you come from; it's where you're going that counts." – **Ella Fitzgerald**

22. "I've been poor, and I've been rich, and rich is better."
 – **Bessie Smith**

23. "I always wanted to be somebody. If I made it, it's half because I was game enough to take a lot of punishment along the way and half because there were a lot of people who cared enough to help me." – **Althea Gibson**

24. "Keep working hard and you can get anything that you want. If God gave you the talent, you should go for it. But don't think it's going to be easy. It's hard!" – **Aaliyah**

25. "Ask for what you want and be prepared to get it."
– **Maya Angelou**

26. "We are all gifted. That is our inheritance." – **Ethel Waters**

27. "Success is liking yourself, liking what you do, and liking how you do it." – **Maya Angelou**

QUOTES THAT EMPHASIZE BLACK AWARENESS

1. "I am very proud to be black but black is not all I am that's my cultural historical background my genetic makeup but it's not all of who I am nor is it the basis from which I answer every question." - **Denzel Washington**

2. "Diversity is not about how we differ diversity of is about embracing one another's uniqueness or Joseph there are no secrets to success it is the result of preparation hard work and learning from failure." - **Colin Powell**

3. "This is a wonderful planet and it is being completely destroyed by people who have too much money and power and no empathy." - **Alice Walker**

4. "It's easier to build strong children than to repair broken men." - **Frederick Douglass**

5. "History has shown us that courage can be contagious, and hope can take on a life of its own." - **Michelle Obama**

6. "Racial superiority is a mere pigment of the imagination author unknown for I am my mother's daughter in the drums of Africa still beat in my heart." - **Mary McLeod Bethune**

7. "The only tired I was, was tired of giving in." - **Rosa Parks**

8. "In recognizing the humanity of black history, we must learn to live together as brothers or perish together as fools." - **Martin Luther King Jr**.

9. "Women if the soul of the nation is to be saved I believe that you must become its old." - **Coretta Scott King**

10. "Never be limited by other people's Limited. One day our descendants will think it's incredible that we paid so much attention to things like the amount of melanin in our skin or the shape of our eyes are our gender instead of the unique identities of each of us as complex human beings." - **Franklin A. Thomas**

NOTABLE QUOTES TO STIMULATE YOUR THOUGHTS

1. "The impatient idealist says: 'Give me a place to stand and I shall move the earth.' But such a place does not exist. We all have to stand on the earth itself and go with her at her pace." - **Chinua Achebe** *(No Longer at Ease)*

2. "Anyone who has ever struggled with poverty knows how extremely expensive it is to be poor." -**James Baldwin** *(Fifth Avenue, Uptown. Esquire)*

3. "To know how much there is to know is the beginning of learning to live." -**Dorothy West** *(The Richer, the Poorer)*

4. "I am an invisible man...I am a man of substance, of flesh and bone, fiber and liquids—and I might even be said to possess a mind. I am invisible, understand, simply because people refuse to see me." - **Ralph Ellison** *(Invisible Man)*

5. "For while the tale of how we suffer, and how we are delighted, and how we may triumph is never new, it always must be heard. There isn't any other tale to tell, it's the only light we've got in all this darkness." - **James Baldwin** *(Sonny's Blues)*

6. "As long as we are not ourselves, we will try to be what other people are." - **Malidoma Patrice Somé** *(Of Water and the Spirit)*

7. "Healing begins where the wound was made." - **Alice Walker** *(The Way Forward Is with a Broken Heart)*

8. "When you know your name, you should hang on to it, for unless it is noted down and remembered, it will die when you do." -**Toni Morrison** *(Song of Solomon)*

9. "If one is lucky, a solitary fantasy can totally transform one million realities." -**Maya Angelou** *(The Heart of a Woman)*

10. "Not everything that is faced can be changed; but nothing can be changed until it is faced." - **James Baldwin** *(As Much Truth As One Can Bear, New York Times)*

11. "Oppressive language does more than represent violence; it is violence; does more than represent the limits of knowledge; it limits knowledge." -**Toni Morrison** *(Nobel lecture, 1993)*

12. "Miracles happen all the time. We're here, aren't we?" - **Marilyn Nelson** *(Abba Jacob and Miracles)*

13. "Ignorance, allied with power, is the most ferocious enemy justice can have." - **James Baldwin** *(No Name in the Street)*

14. "Nobody's as powerful as we make them out to be." - **Alice Walker** *(The Third Life of Grange Copeland)*

IN CONCLUSION...

I hope you have been inspired by my selection of quotes. My goal was to include "something for everyone," no matter what your age, gender or ethnicity. Most importantly, to me, is that **Quotes and Anecdotes** has sent a message to young people striving for something they believed could be obtained, by dreaming big and making the grade. I believe that no matter how long it takes, *if you stick with something long enough, something always happens.*

Regardless of what you do in life, *always* keep it real with yourself. Being honest about who you are and your circumstances will keep your mind focused and your feet sure. You can't change anyone but yourself, so acknowledge your position for *exactly* what it is, accept it no matter how much it hurts, and then take steps to improve your situation. I have come to realize that the way to do that is through education, hard work, dedication and determination. Begin to try to help yourself before you can help others.

While writing **Quotes and Anecdotes** I decided to use the same principles that are relevant to the "Make the Grade Foundation" – parents, teachers, students, community, spirituality, health and financial literacy. Here are my final thoughts about each principle:

PARENTS

I am a firm believer of the mindset that "it takes a village to raise a child." Whether children are raised in a 1-parent or 2-parent household, a 1-gender or 2-gender household, or by grandparents or foster parents, the parenting role is vitally important to either the progression or detriment of the child. Nine times out of ten, children will emulate the adults that surround them. Powerful women, as mother figures, greatly influence the young ones in their care by teaching them about compassion and values. Strong men, as father figures who are always present in a child's life, contribute to the child's esteem and steadfastness that can lead to a more positive society.

TEACHERS

I applaud every teacher, who leads the way for our children from kindergarten to college, giving them a promise of a better education and a brighter future. To every teacher, I celebrate you as you continue to do the hard work that is necessary to guide our young people in the right direction for the edification of their young minds that can grow and become valuable to this generation and those to come. Thank you for your integrity and dedication.

STUDENTS

In the entertainment business, I meet a lot of people that you hear on the radio and see on TV. They all have one thing in common – they are on a mission to eat, sleep and breathe success. Don't be afraid to try something that appears to be a challenge. Failure is good because it helps you to learn by your mistakes. If you stick with something long enough, something always happens…just make sure it is positive. And always remember that what you are is God's gift to you. What you make of yourself is your gift to God. So, choose your choice and let your choice control the chooser. Find out what you want to do in life and stick with it.

COMMUNITY

An Incredible Teacher · Mentor · Friend, Hal Jackson, taught me the importance of Community Service, he would often say, *"It's nice to be important, but it's more important to be nice."* He was always concerned with how people felt. Hal's wisdom, compassion and mentorship helped me to realize the importance of community service and allowed me to understand that everyone I would meet would be important to me. I challenge you to be a good leader. Our younger people are looking up to you to lead them in the right direction. If they see you doing something wrong, they are going to do it too. A kind word, gesture or deed can make a difference in someone's life every day.

SPIRITUALITY

No matter what your religion or how you worship…Have Faith, Seek your Blessings, Ask for Favor and Pray daily…your life will change. "Ask, and it will be given to you." (Matthew 7:7) God has given you all the blessings that you could ever want or need. But, you must activate them, if you don't ask for and use His blessings you will forfeit them.

HEALTH

Energize your mind and body every day. Feed it with positive thoughts and nourish it with healthy food. When your body is healthy it energizes you and usually triggers more wholesome activities that can be beneficial to you and to those people you come in contact with. Whether you're a student or working on your career goals, being in the best-possible physical and mental health will influence your outcome and contribute to your success.

FINANCIAL LITERACY

If you do nothing else with your money, once you tend to your personal needs, I encourage you to give back where it counts. Even if you are living paycheck to paycheck, figure out a way to allocate a small fraction of your funds to someone less fortunate than you. Helping other people, donating to a charitable organization or cause, or tithing can be very rewarding in ways that are unimaginable. When you realize that you are able to help someone less fortunate than you, an awareness that you can do even more might be triggered. With that awareness, the dream begins and with that dream the reality happens.

Your Daily Dose of Quotes and Anecdotes

ABOUT THE AUTHOR

DOCTOR BOB LEE

"Doctor" Bob Lee is one of the most recognized entertainment personalities in New York. For more than 30 years, he's had a rewarding career as a Radio and TV personality, DJ, author, motivational speaker, consultant and entrepreneur. Lee started out as a DJ for 88,7 WT NY Radio in 1978 while he attended the New York Institute of Technology, where he later received his BA and MA in Communications. Lee eventually went on to be music director, program director and general manager for WTNY. He also started Doctor Bob Lee & Company, a mobile-DJ business where he traveled to colleges and universities to play, cut and mix/blend recorded music for numerous celebrations. In 1980, Lee joined 107.5 WBLS as an intern. In 1981, he won the Top DJ Award for 98.7 KISS-FM.

Soon after, in 1981, Lee was offered a job with WBLS, where he has since had an exciting and diverse career. For eight years, Lee hosted the weekend edition of WBLS's renowned program the Quiet Storm under legendary DJ Vaughn Harper. He interviewed the likes of Michelle Obama and musical greats such as Stevie Wonder, Patti LaBelle, Luther Vandross, Beyonce, Mariah Carey, Mary J. Blige, Kenny "Baby Face" Edmonds, Wynton Marsalis, Whitney Houston, Alicia Keys, Jill Scott, and many more.

Bob Lee started the Daily Dose on 107.5 WBLS and 1190 WLIB, which converted to Bob Lee's Digital Dose where you can log in and connect to the latest in lifestyle and healthcare tips from health professionals. The Digital Dose focuses on topics such as heart disease, diabetes and other ailments common to people in our community. Bob started the WBLS On Time Program with Ken "Spider" Webb in the Morning, as a vehicle to encourage students to Stay in School and Be on Time. Since then, he has a key reporting role with every Morning Show host, from Ken Webb up to its current host, Steve Harvey.

Bob has provided special live reports on the Morning Show for "9/11", the "New York City Marathon", various parades and other special events, and hundreds of WBLS-sponsored community programs.

As part of his community-based work, Lee has developed strong ties to many local and national politicians and public figures, including President Clinton, Mayor Bill de Blasio, Mayor Michael Bloomberg, Mayor David Dinkins, and Bronx Borough President Ruben Diaz Jr. For more than ten years, Lee has hosted the weekly live television program "Open", which broadcasts on BronxNet, and is viewed worldwide. The program features news and topics affecting our community and also treats viewers to new and established musical guests. He also hosts The Bob Lee Show, a music-intensive radio show. In addition to his on-air roles, Lee manages community affairs and government relations for WBLS and WLIB.

Lee does appearances frequently throughout the five boroughs and Tri-state area as the host of various events, such as the Wingate Field Concerts in Brooklyn, Jacob Javits Convention Center, Madison Square Garden, Barclay Center in Brooklyn, Summer Stages and the Apollo Theater. His strong ties to the community are reflected in his many charitable endeavors. He's the President & CEO of the Make the Grade Foundation, a non-profit organization that provides mentoring and aid to school children.

About the Author

This motivated him to write **Seven Ways to Make the Grade** an autobiographical, motivational book partnering with parent, teacher, student, clergy, community, financial literacy and health organizations, to help guide people on their life's journey.

He's also the President & CEO of Bob Lee Enterprises, an umbrella for his many talents including, DJing, motivational speaking, coaching and consulting for companies who want to do grassroots promotions. Lee also helps college students interested in radio careers. He served as a mentor for "Table for Two", a weekly music program broadcasting from 88.1 FM WLIU in Brooklyn staffed by interns from Long Island University.

Your Daily Dose of Quotes and Anecdotes is Bob Lee's second published book.

Follow Doctor Bob Lee on:
Facebook, Twitter, Instagram

YOUR FAVORITE QUOTE(S)

About the Author

Your Daily Dose of Quotes and Anecdotes

About the Author

Your Daily Dose of Quotes and Anecdotes

About the Author

Your Daily Dose of Quotes and Anecdotes

About the Author

Your Daily Dose of Quotes and Anecdotes

About the Author

www.ingramcontent.com/pod-product-compliance
Lightning Source LLC
Chambersburg PA
CBHW070549010526
44118CB00012B/1268